C0-ABO-246

Mysterious Ireland

Sheila St. Clair's first serious investigation into the world of the paranormal was in the 1960s and thirty years later she is still travelling on her journey of discovery which has been interspersed by lectures, articles, regular weekly broadcasting on radio and appearances on television in her capacity as one of Ireland's best-known authorities on ESP, telepathic communication, apparitions and poltergeist activity. She lives in Lisburn, County Antrim.

Mysterious Ireland

SHEILA ST. CLAIR

ROBERT HALE · LONDON

© *Sheila St. Clair 1994*
First published in Great Britain 1994

ISBN 0 7090 5528 5

Robert Hale Limited
Clerkenwell House
Clerkenwell Green
London EC1R 0HT

The right of Sheila St. Clair to be identified as
author of this work has been asserted by her
in accordance with the Copyright, Designs and
Patents Act 1988.

2   4   6   8   10   9   7   5   3   1

Photoset in North Wales by
Derek Doyle & Associates, Mold, Clwyd.
Printed in Great Britain by
St Edmundsbury Press Ltd, Bury St Edmunds, Suffolk.
Bound by WBC Ltd, Bridgend, Mid-Glamorgan.

Contents

With happy memories of my friend
Patrick M.

Acknowledgements

May I thank the large number of folk who wrote, telephoned or made time to give me information about 'mysterious Ireland'. Their contribution to this book is too great to fully acknowledge properly. My thanks, too, to my friends Tom Turley, Tom Porter and Linda Ballard, as well as my colleagues in the media who, with information and practical advice, encouraged me on my way. I owe a special vote of thanks to my husband, Stanley Wyllie, who patiently trailed me all over the thirty-two counties, camera in hand. I only hope that in some small fashion I have fulfilled their expectations!

I also wish to extend my thanks to the Linenhall Library, Belfast, Lisburn Library, County Antrim, and the Folk Museum, Cultra, County Down.

Sheila St. Clair. January, 1994.

Key

1 **Donegal**
Glenade Lake
Bansidhe

2 **Londonderry**
Death Coach (an caoiste bodhar)
Springhill

3 **Antrim**
Dunluce Castle
Garron Tower
O'Neill Bansidhe
Piper's Hill, Lisburn
Invermore House, Larne
Bonamargy Abbey, Ballycastle
Carrickfergus Castle

4 **Tyrone**
Coonian Ghost
Burning Cottage, Strabane
Tempo Manor
Haunted Greyhound

5 **Down**
Narrow Water Castle
Druid's Circle
Finnebrogue Gates
Gillhall, Dromore
Greyabbey, Apparitions
Haddock's ghost, Drumbeg
Inch Abbey
Grey lady, Lambeg

6 **Armagh**

7 **Monaghan**

8 **Fermanagh**
Castle Archdale
Derrygonnelly poltergeist
Tully Castle
White Light of Crom

9 **Louth**

10 **Leitrim**

11 **Cavan**

12 **Meath**
Battle of Boyne
Gormanstown Foxes
Skyrne Castle

13 **Sligo**
Lissadell House
Rathmoy House
Sligo Road

14 **Roscommon**

15 **Longford**

16 **Westmeath**
Emo House

17 **Kildare**
Clangowes Wood

18 **Dublin**
Bansidhe, Grand Canal
'Ireland's Eye'
Killucan
Lucan
Malahide Castle
Rathfarnham Castle
Monkstown
St Patrick's Cathedral
Tymon Castle

19 **Wicklow**
Glenmalure
Hellfire Club
Killakee House
Poulaphouca (fairy horse)

20 **Carlow**
Huntingdon Castle – Clonegal

21 **Leix**

22 **Offaly**
Clonony Castle
Leap Castle

23 **Galway**
Inchy, Gort
Yeats' Tower, Ballylee
Renvyle House

24 **Mayo**
Bellacorick Bridge
Killeadon House
Kiltimagh
Phantom Bugler, Castlebar

25 **Clare**
Quin Abbey

26 **Tipperary**
Horses of Longfield (Bianconi)
Orloff Whip

27 **Kilkenny**

28 **Wexford**
Enniscorthy
Rineen Hill
Tintern Abbey
Loftus Hall
Moretown Massacre

29 **Waterford**

30 **Cork**
Bandon
Charles Fort
Doneraile
Drimshallon Park
Drumshambo
Kilcolman or Spencer's
    Castle
Killeshandra
Middletown
Doneraile
Spike Island

31 **Kerry**
Dun An Òir

Introduction

The political and sectarian divisions of Ireland tend to be better known than those that constitute the real and material island of Ireland. Its geographical conformation and historical boundaries are, thankfully, to some people of more importance than the perpetual struggle of 'orange and green'. But Ireland is more than just a sum of its parts, whether they be political, historical or geographical. It has a spirit and a personality of its own that over the centuries has breathed a particular life into its hills and valleys, its people and places. It is also a land of paradoxes and conundrums, not easily understood in the cold light of the everyday. Those of us who know it fairly well are aware that it is a place full of light and serenity that can turn only too easily to darkness and brooding passions; a mysterious and infuriating part of God's creation where the Past and the Present continually jostle for priority, where Yesterday and Today become inextricably melded together so that one is never sure where one ends and the other begins.

In basic terms, Ireland is quite easy to come to understand. The political divisions mean that the northern end of the island has an area of six counties known as 'Northern Ireland', while the rest of the island is divided into twenty-six counties known as the Republic of Ireland. Overlapping both British and Irish territory are four provinces that ignore national boundaries: they are Ulster, Munster, Leinster and Connaught. Of these, three are wholly within the Republic, while Northern Ireland possesses six out of the nine counties of Ulster. It is not uncommon to hear Northern Ireland referred to as 'the six counties'. The whole of Ireland is contained within 2,000 miles of coastline, with the North Channel on one side and the coasts of Scotland and Wales on the other. The whole effect of the land mass, with its central core of limestone and its liberal sprinkling

11

of rivers and lochs, is like that of a saucer, which in turn is dominated by the course of Ireland's longest river, the Shannon, its two hundred mile length covering a fifth of the whole country.

For the archaeologist, the artist, the historian and the scholar, Ireland holds a wealth of experience and information dating back into the mists of prehistory. It is an undeniably beautiful place, yet below that smiling and alluring countenance lies another Ireland, possessed of a dark and turbulent spirit that can participate in otherworldly events. The mystical side of Ireland is bound up in deep racial traditions and cultures, born of people whose religious faith goes back to before the Druids. With the coming of Patrick and the growth of Christianity, another powerful tradition took root and flourished. Yet through all this the Elder Faiths still held sway, the magical tradition of the Faerie was still regarded as important and the belief in the world of the paranormal is as strong today as it ever was. Ireland is a land of mystery, one could even say of 'sinister' influences at times. She is the 'dark Rosaleen' of her many poets.

Some aspects of the paranormal are stronger than others in this island. It is said that the Irish are a 'haunted people', as opposed to the Anglo-Saxon races and their preponderance of 'haunted places'. There is a strong apprehension of death and the rites of passage. Death warnings feature in much of the Irish folklore from bansidhe to black coaches; poltergeist manifestation is a very strong tradition all over Ireland, and some of the best documentation of poltergeist phenomena come from this part of the world. Ireland also has its fair share of apparitional beings and haunted houses, of mysterious lights and knockings. Some of the information about such experiences has been handed down from generation to generation; other strange phenomena has a recent foundation in both town and country. The writer who said that 'millions of spiritual creatures walk the earth unseen, both while we sleep and while we wake' must assuredly have been thinking of Ireland.

The Republic of Ireland

1   The Black Coach of Killeshandra

We start our search for 'mysterious Ireland' in her second smallest county, Carlow, which only covers about 350 square miles. There are many places of historic interest in Carlow, including Muin Bheag (small thicket), whose castle Ballymoon is now a ruin but was originally one of the earliest Anglo-Norman strongholds built in Ireland and dates from the fourteenth century.

A sister castle to Ballymoon that attracts much attention from those who are interested in the paranormal is Clonegal or Huntingdon Castle, as it became known in later times. This castle stands on the River Derry near the Wexford border. Its name 'Cluan na nGall' means 'the meadow of the stranger'.

The castle itself was built by the Esmond family in 1625 and is presently the family home of the Durdin-Robertsons. The castle has many interesting features, including a holy well sited within the castle itself. On an adjoining piece of land there is a large bullaun stone made of granite that acts as a focus for healing those afflicted by warts. In early times the stone was used for the grinding of corn, and as a result it has a shallow depression at its centre. Rain water collects in this depression and is used to bathe the warts.

The back avenue to the castle is said to be haunted by Maeve, Queen of Connaught, and contains the so-called 'spy bush', a holy bush looking down over the river and valley. Here the apparition of a 'White Lady' has been seen combing her hair in the moonlight. Sometimes she is also accompanied by a white cat. Whether this truly is the apparition of Maeve or one of the 'sidhe' (fairy) is a matter for conjecture. The famous 800-year-old Yew Tree Walk is said to be haunted by Franciscan friars, the site having monastic connections from early times.

Within the castle itself there has been evidence of aetheric echoes, the implication of which is the ability of the aether to retain sounds of everyday happenings, in the fashion of a tape recording. Examples of the aetherics of Clonegal include a conversation 'recorded' in a chimney, regarding a dispute over domestic bills and, some time earlier, another conversation heard by children in the attic, consisting of a discussion between a recruit and some other soldiers, making reference to a time when the castle was garrisoned. Other 'echoes' are more recent: the sounds of a typewriter and the disconnection of electrical appliances have been heard in areas where it would have been perfectly logical for them to have occurred, even though the objects themselves were not there at the time the 'echoes' were heard.

The castle has its share of apparitional materializations too. In one of the large and imposing bedrooms the apparition of Bishop Leslie (of the Monaghan Leslies) was seen by a visitor. A white-wigged man sometimes appears from the powder closet in the Red Bedroom, seemingly to 'inspect' visitors who may be staying overnight! A family member visiting the castle saw a woman he took to be a housekeeper in a downstairs passage where, to his consternation, she brushed a book to the floor from a bookcase – and promptly vanished. The haunted Red Room once had a materialization of a 'nurse' dressed in a white apron and wearing a swan brooch on her dress. She appeared to be taking an interest in a small child that had been put to bed in the room for a rest. She was seen again a second time in broad daylight, this time by an astonished mother who saw her standing beside the bed 'taking care of' the woman's child.

On a rather more unnerving plane, one of the nieces of the Durdin-Robertsons saw in the Yellow Room a tiny hand floating in the air, while Olivia Durdin-Robertson, the mistress of the castle, felt a tiny hand in hers as she lay in bed in an 'out of the body state', a form of sensory consciousness extending beyond the physical body.

From a gracious castle and home in County Carlow we go to a small village in County Cavan, Killeshandra, one of the areas in Ireland where the spectacular manifestation known as 'the Black coach' or 'an caoiste bodhar' has been witnessed. Ireland is full of information about death warnings, from knockings or rappings to the 'Black coach', one of the most feared. It is a phenomenon which has also been reported outside Ireland in other parts of the British isles, including the west of England and Welsh borders. The Black Coach of Killeshandra, however, is one of the best documented.

Killeshandra is situated to the west of Lough Oughter, which has several other small loughs close by. As a matter of interest, the ancestors of Edgar Allen Poe came from the district. While there are many reports of 'the black or dead' coach being seen about Ireland, few are as well authenticated as Killeshandra, not least because it has several unusual features.

In the first instance, the coach appears to date back to prehistoric times. It appears at irregular intervals and only seems to travel a limited distance. Sometimes – and it may well be only a coincidence – the coach will appear at the time of a death in the locality. It keeps irregular hours, and if confronted by a witness on the road it will either rush past at a headlong pace or go into reverse and simply disappear.

The name 'Killeshandra' also presents an enigma, for it can be translated as 'the Church of the Old Rath' or as 'the Wood of the old Rath of the Druids'. The latter is held to be more likely, as from ancient times the place was looked upon as a powerful sacred site, prior to the coming of Patrick and the introduction of Christianity. The interest in the actual meaning of the name is important in relation to the history of the black coach itself. If local tradition is correct, the coach dates back to Druidic times, when their rites and ceremonies were practised beneath the oaks beside Croghan Lake. That the rath itself was a centre of worship may well be true and, more gruesomely, it has been said that the black coach was used in those times to convey victims to the place of sacrifice. The area is full of the remains of sacred sites. The great temple of the druids, the Moy Slaught, lay only a few miles westward. Thus it seems a viable theory that, from time to time, the black coach may travel its old routes, where once white-robed priest and garlanded victim came together at the place of sacrifice.

Nearer to our time, the evidence for the black coach was carefully set down by a Protestant minister, the Rev. J.H. Whitsitt, who lived for over twenty years in the manse at Killeshandra. He was known as an honest and popular man throughout the district, with an informed interest in local folklore. Croghan Manse was but a mile from Killeshandra on the Ballyconnell Road, and both church and manse stood on ground of some significance, close to the point where the Croghan River enters the lake. Beyond lay a hill, the crowning place of the O'Rourke Chiefs. It was in front of the church that Mr Whitsitt saw the black coach.

It was a cold, wintry night and the minister was alone at the manse working in his study. When the clock struck ten, on impulse he went into the sitting-room to see if there was any sign of his family returning from a visit. The night was clear with snow lying crisp on the ground. As Mr Whitsitt stood at the window he saw a light turning onto the Ballyconnell Road, about a quarter of a mile away. The light and the movement of it suggested a coach and the minister was somewhat surprised that the coach was lit, as at that time in the latter part of the nineteenth century there were no specific regulations about 'lighting up' on a clear night. The coach came closer, turning the corner of the road and coming directly towards the manse itself. It was at this point that Mr Whitsitt began to feel distinctly uneasy, for as the vehicle came closer he could see neither horses nor driver, simply a long black coach. As the astonished clergyman watched, the lights gradually receded, although still shining as brightly as before, until the vehicle vanished altogether around a bend in the road. The direction it took was towards Aughbawn.

Mr Whitsitt was confronted by the coach again, about a year after the first visitation. This time the minister was coming home after a parochial visit and he and his stable lad were in the yard, putting up the horse, when the gable end of the stables was lit by a brilliant light, and both master and boy heard the sound of wheels on the road. The coach performed the same circuit as before, coming down the road as far as the church and then reversing back the way it had come. The only significant difference for the alarmed Mr Whitsitt was that this time he heard the sound of wheels.

While the minister could give no adequate explanation of what he had seen, he was no doubt relieved when he learned that a near neighbour had also seen the black coach but in much more alarming circumstances.

In the case of Frank McGovern of Aughbawn, Killeshandra, he and a friend had been travelling along the Newtowngore

Road one evening and heard behind them the sound of wheels. On looking over their shoulders, they both saw the coach. To avoid being run down by it, the two men quite literally threw themselves into the ditch. The coach passed alongside them and the terrified men saw it quite clearly. They told witnesses that it was 'tall and black' and there was 'a man seated on the box', but while he appeared to be holding reins in his hands there were no horses and the coach, as far as they could see, was empty. A short time after passing them, the coach did a sharp right turn through a hedge and vanished from sight.

It has been noted that the Newtowngore Road was often the road where the coach had been seen; it may have some bearing that this was the most direct route to Moy Slaught. The reports of other witnesses all tally very closely with those of Mr Whitsitt and Frank McGovern.

One other witness, a man from Aughawilliam, County Leitrim, also had a unique encounter with the Killeshandra coach. He was bringing home stock from the fair at Blacklion very late. The night was wet and wild, and such heavy rain began to fall that, as they entered Killeshandra Town, he and his helper took shelter under the arches of the market house. As they sheltered, they heard the noise of a heavy vehicle on the street coming towards them. The bemused men could scarcely believe their eyes when they saw something that only superficially resembled a coach. The men described it thus: 'It seemed more like a box or a chest than a coach. It was about four feet in height and carried no lights, nor was there a light coming from inside. It passed quite close, no more than four or five yards from us, but we could see no sign of horse or driver, nor could we see any wheels. It made a great noise as it passed the Market House, and vanished up the street, and after that we saw no more of it ...'

Mr James Roche, who gave this account, told a tale substantially different from any other about the coach and, interestingly, while others had not seen the vehicle, they had heard it. There were a number of local inhabitants who had heard the rumble of the wheels and the sound of horses. A dozen or more respectable men and women had cowered in the hedges about Killeshandra as the wind of an invisible coach passed them by. There were, mercifully, few reports of the black coach having any connection with human tragedy.

One of the most poignant reports came from a family sitting with their dying child. Several members of the family heard the sound of a coach or carriage driving up to the front door. It so happened that the elderly mother also living in the house was far from well, and her daughter-in-law remarked to a guest 'that she knew who the coach had come for', indicating the old lady. The woman thus addressed by her hostess happened to be the wife of the Rev. Whitsitt, and she was certainly likely to remember the conversation and the incident. Later that day, however, it was the child, not the ailing grandmother, who died.

In this case, one must assume that the black coach of Killeshandra was also fulfilling the function of 'an caoiste bodhar', the 'death coach', although such incidents were rare. The black coach was seen up to 1910, but since that time there have been no further reports of its strange and sinister journeyings.

Coaches also figure largely in and about Bunratty Castle in County Clare, one of the most famous and well preserved castles in Ireland. But unlike Killeshandra, these coaches are strictly the sleek and comfortable 'monsters' of the twentieth century that, every season, line the road outside the castle demesne, bringing visitors from all over the world.

Bunratty is one of Ireland's best fortified places, an imposing structure which fully satisfies the visitor's ideas of what one might expect as an illustration of Ireland's embattled past. Yet no matter how many times one comes upon it beside the road to Limerick City, one cannot fail to be impressed by its sheer size and majestic stance.

In the mid-fourteenth century there was probably a wooden structure here belonging to a Norman knight, Robert De Muscegros. Beside this structure, a town with regular fairs and a market grew up to make Bunratty a place of some importance.

After the death of De Muscegros, Edward I granted the lands to Thomas De Clare, who built a stone castle in 1277. Thomas was the great-great-grandson of Strongbow and Eva McMurrough. One of the bloodier deeds which took place at Bunratty was the slaughter of Brien Ruaddh O Brien by De Clare, after they had pledged their mutual friendship under the seal of the Sacraments. Other unsavoury details tell of O Brien being torn apart by horses, then decapitated and his body hanged at the castle gate.

And so it was that a royal feud was born between the O Briens and the De Clares. The castle was attacked several times, both by O Briens and Macnamaras, and it was set on fire on at least two occasions before 1306. The castle was rebuilt, but during the reign of Edward II it was razed yet again. By the 1450s it was rebuilt and under the control of Maccon Macsioda Macnamara. Then the castle was gifted to the O Briens, possibly by marriage settlement, so that by the middle of the sixteenth century Bunratty was ruled powerfully and well by Murragh O Brien, who, upon making his submission to Henry VIII, was created Earl of Thomond.

During the Great Rebellion of 1641 the castle languished under both Royalist and Commonwealth military and by decrees was spared the terrible violence of the times. By 1720 the estate was acquired by William Stoddart, who made it into a family residence and was able to rehabilitate much of the old castle building. Fortunately for us, we now can see the restoration of a large part of this bloodstained relic of a turbulent past.

Inside the castle are many beautiful artefacts, including the great Armada Table, salvaged from the flagship by Boethius Clancy, High Sheriff of Clare, and given to his brother-in-law, Conor O Brien, and the beautiful ciborium of Hungarian gilt and enamel set with precious stones. Such treasures exist in an atmosphere that comes drifting up from the past and reaches out in faint echoes that permeate the narrow winding stairs and small dark chambers.

In one such chamber in the 1970s, a young girl, pausing on the worn stone stair and peering curiously into a room, saw seated at a table a man in ruff and breeches, writing in a book. He seemed wholly preoccupied and totally oblivious to the fact that he had a visitor. The girl, thinking that he was one of the castle custodial staff in costume, waited for him to greet her. When he did not, the girl, feeling a trifle disappointed and faintly apprehensive, moved on to the next floor. Here she commented to one of the staff on duty about the man in the room below who had chosen to ignore her. In any case, she wanted to know, who did this man represent?

The member of staff was puzzled and assured her that they had no tableaux set up in the castle, and that she must have been mistaken. The girl was quite emphatic about what she had seen and gave the staff member a minute description of the man at the desk. She also repeated the description to friends who by then had joined her. They revisited the room, where all the furniture was as she had described – except that no gentleman in ruff and breeches now sat on the chair at the desk.

From time to time, small tales such as this filter out from individuals on a visit to Bunratty. Less frequently, the staff will catch a hint of 'something' that they may prefer not to dwell on, especially if they are alone in the castle after the visitors have gone. A small and simple incident, for example, was that of one member of staff who saw the small figure of a girl walking below in the Great Hall. She was carrying a pile of dishes, and then disappeared with her load out onto the stair. The watcher knew that he alone had access to that particular part of the castle and, in any case, his female counterpart did not come to work in a grey stuff gown and a white mob cap! The author herself, on a visit to Bunratty, had the overwhelming compulsion to step aside on one of the narrow stairs as 'someone' or something pushed past her.

Bunratty is very evocative, and even the most blasé of guests will sometimes feel the faintest of breaths on their cheek, or the lightest of touches as they descend the winding stairs. For 900 years this castle has known love and war, victory and defeat. It has been in the grip of powerful emotions that make a nonsense of logic and of our world of the micro chip and computer. 'Solid fact' may be the lode star of the twentieth century, but in the shadows of Bunratty one wonders uneasily what other considerations must be taken into account.

Another spot in County Clare, much quieter and less public than Bunratty, is the village of Quin. It is a very picturesque place with its famous Franciscan Friary that is remarkably well preserved. The Abbey of Quin was built by Sioda Macnamara in 1402 for the Franciscan Order. He had chosen the site well, for it incorporated within itself the great Anglo-Norman stronghold of the De Clare. Three of the castle towers stand at the angles of the conventual building. The high altar and cloisters are complete together with other buildings at ground level, while the slender tower of the abbey church soars above the swift grey waters of the river.

The Friary was suppressed in 1541, but the friars continued to live in the district until the beginning of the nineteenth century. Apart from the great abbey ruins, there is much of historical interest in the surrounding area. One can see the ruins of several castles from the top of the abbey tower, including Dangan Castle, said to be the oldest Anglo-Norman fortress in Munster. On the road from Quin to Tulla is a mound – Ma Adhair – on which the Dalcassian Kings were crowned prior to the reign of Elizabeth I. Here, at this place of green grass and grey stone, the centuries meet in a mixture of prayerful silence and the faintly echoing clash of arms. Quin Abbey is a strange and brooding place and one is very conscious of the tread of one's feet in the silence and the close proximity of the ashes of the past. There is that uneasy feeling of being watched by the sleepers beneath the rough grass.

Strange tales are told about this remote and sacred site. One such tale comes from a nineteenth century traveller who, trudging along the road one autumn evening, saw as he looked over the fields towards the Abbey in the fading light a small body of men, their heads bowed and covered and led by a crucifer, heading for the Abbey entrance. He also heard, faint on the evening air, the solemn notes of vespers. As he fell to his knees on the narrow muddied track, he prayed as he had not prayed for many a long year, a prayer for the repose of the souls of those humble and God-fearing men.

Another account from Quin comes from a young boy who, hiding terrified in the shadow of the Abbey, saw older shades than those seen by the nineteenth century traveller. The boy saw two shadowy fighting men, mounted on great horses, match blow for blow in a silent struggle, re-enacting some ancient battle. And in numerous individual recollections men and women of our own time have heard, in a heart stopping moment, the ghostly sound of the Abbey bell calling the faithful to prayer.

From 1402 to the present century is a great leap in time, but there is one small incident that has been well attested to by witnesses up until the present day at a place not far from Lahinch, County Clare, known as Rineen Hill. This hill was the site of a skirmish between the British troops and the Irish during the 'troubles' in 1916. It was a fierce encounter by all accounts and most of the British troops were killed. The bodies were laid out near the hill for identification, and then removed for burial.

In recent times, campers who have pitched their tents near to the spot have found that during the night there would be some 'disturbance' accompanied by a wind that would uproot their tents and toss their belongings about. Those thus treated were usually wise enough to take the hint and find an alternative camp site!

This incident is similar to what happened in Glenmalure, County Wicklow, which was the site for two earlier affrays. In 1580, and again in 1798, great slaughter occurred, and those stopping in the Glen overnight have found themselves involved in disturbances and have seen camp-fire lights. One may assume that the relaxed atmosphere of holiday camping may make some people vulnerable to heightened extrasensory perception, and they may as a result respond to echoes from the past. While no positive connection can be made between what happened at Rineen Hill and Glenmalure, it does give pause for thought.

2   The Phantom Pack

Doneraile in County Cork is notable for two events of interest, the first to the lovers of literature and the second to those who have an interest in the paranormal. With regard to the former, three miles to the north of the town are the ruins of Kilcolman or Spenser's Castle, a small pele tower where for eight years Edmund Spenser wrote some of the most immortal poetry in the English language, including at least three books of *The Faerie Queene*.

A loyal servant of Elizabeth I, Spenser was given 3,000 acres of the land escheated to the Crown after the crushing of the Desmond rebellion, together with the castle of Kilcolman. It was here in 1589 that Walter Raleigh visited him and persuaded him to take *The Faerie Queene* to London, where the poem was published in 1590.

Kilcolman was attacked in 1598, and while Spenser and his wife escaped, their young son perished in the flames. In 1852 another writer was linked with Doneraile. His name was Canon Sheehan, an Irish writer mainly noted for his work dealing with Irish clerical life and its social relationships in the nineteenth century.

In terms of Doneraile's connections with the paranormal, the story of 'the phantom pack' of the family of Lord Doneraile came into prominence in the 1830s. One night in the 1830s, one of Lord Doneraile's keepers was crossing the Home Park with his young son, doing the nightly rounds which included checking the gates into the park. Suddenly his attention was drawn to the sound of the baying of a pack of hounds. The noise seemed to be coming from somewhere very close and certainly within the confines of the park, despite the fact that no hounds were kept there.

His first thought was that a pack of hounds, kennelled some

distance down the country road alongside the demesne, had somehow managed to stray into the park, though how this could occur through locked gates puzzled him. Then, out of the shadows on the far side of the park, he saw a pack of hounds running in full cry.

Although they ran very close to him, neither the keeper nor his son heard any sound save from one or two stragglers who gave tongue intermittently. Hard on the heels of the hounds came a tall distinguished man on a fine bay horse. No sound came at all from horse and rider. Suddenly the whole pack and rider swerved around the edge of the plantation and disappeared from view. The keeper, now thoroughly unnerved, attempted to fathom how horse and hounds, together with the mysterious rider, had managed to circumnavigate the gates as easily on exiting as on their original entry. He knew that it was the closed season for hunting, with the house shut up and the family away.

The next day he made enquiries among estate staff, but no one could account for what he and his son had seen. One or two of the grooms in the stable yard did admit to hearing tales that the park was haunted by an earlier Lord Doneraile, but no one else had actually witnessed the event.

At this point the whole affair excited further comment and letters and reports were written, including certain letters from the Doneraile family. Lord Doneraile himself discounted any personal experience of such an event, as did his mother and his sister, Lady Castletown, though both women claimed some sketchy knowledge of a legend about a 'phantom pack'. Lady Castletown was of the opinion that the 'master' of the pack was the third Lord Doneraile, a man of a 'lively' disposition who was eventually killed in a duel.

Another letter in manuscript form, dated 21 December 1905, and based on information from the Doneraile branch of the St Leger family, expands on the story. In fact it endeavoured to trace the actual route that the 'pack' took. '... the chase goes from Ballydineen via Glou-na-Goth, Wilkinson's Lawn, through Byblox, across the ford at Shangh-agha-Keel to Aghboobleen into Watkin's Glen and thence into the Old Deer Park, the Horse Close and then into the Park proper ...' The informant continued, 'He [the apparition] appears to take great delight in Wilkinson's Lawn, for here it was that a noble stag was lost sight of – and of course it was there it was most sought after ...'

Further information elicited the facts that in the autumn of 1904, two gentlemen going to the fair, leading a fine horse behind their trap, stopped at the iron gates of the park to light their pipes when 'an old gentleman in old style clothes walked through the gates and patted the horse'. Both men recognized 'a member of the St Leger family who they had known'. Other folk who knew the area well talked of the late Lord Doneraile being seen beneath a tree, designated as 'Lord Doneraile's Oak'. Another sighting of 'the noble lord' was given by a man called Reardon, who saw the apparition riding a powerful black horse in the park. His sister, who was with him at the time, saw nothing, but he insisted that he had had to drag her out of the way of the horse and rider. Other estate workers attested to seeing the apparition, including the Doneraile herdsman, Paddy Shea.

There are one or two interesting features with regard to the Doneraile manifestations. One was that the aural phenomena were inconsistent; sometimes the hounds were heard baying while the horse and rider were silent; sometimes galloping hooves were heard but no hounds. In some instances the apparitions did not vanish but merely disappeared from sight. As these events took place mostly in daylight or bright moonlight and the figures seemed to be solid and three dimensional, it was difficult to decide whether the witnesses were caught up in a joint hallucination or were having separate experiences of a telepathic kind. They could have been participating in the recreation of an event that had previously taken place in real terms and thus were exercising a clairvoyant faculty. In most cases the witnesses did not seem unduly alarmed, more surprised or puzzled.

Among Ireland's many castles that suffered under the assaults of Cromwell's men was Wallstown Castle, County Cork, burned down in the summer of 1642. Its owner, Captain Wall, was captured and imprisoned in Cork, where, after much suffering, he died. However, this unfortunate man is not the apparition said to haunt the castle. Instead, it is said to be a man called Harry Bennet, a cavalier. He manifests in a very bizarre fashion. Local tradition has it that 'a man in white' who carries a pole in his hand appears on the public highway and puts the pole down in front of passers-by to deter them. If requested, he will remove the pole and then laugh at his terrified victims. Occasionally local cottagers have had the pole pushed through their cottage windows. One suggestion as to the significance of the pole is that it represents the one on which the cavalier's own head was displayed after his execution.

More tragic but less bizarre, nearly twenty-five years after the razing of Wallstown Castle the then Duke of Ormonde built a military fort at Kinsale, County Cork, destined to become a British military base. The ghostly incident that was to make Charles Fort notorious was that of the haunting of 'the White Lady'. The incident related to the first governor of the fort, a Colonel Warrender, and his daughter, who went by the unusual name of 'Wilful'. The lady married Sir Trevor Ashurst and it was while on their honeymoon that the tragedy occurred. Some accounts state that it happened on the wedding day itself.

The bride expressed a wish to have a posy of some of the pretty wild flowers that grew on the steep face of the rock below the fortress, and an obliging sentry on duty offered to fetch them for her, providing that her new young husband, Sir Trevor, would stand in for him until he returned. Sir Trevor gladly agreed and took over the sentry's rifle and coat, but after a while, due no doubt to an excess of good food and even better drink, Sir Trevor dozed off. The bride's father, Colonel Warrender, who was noted for his strict discipline, decided to 'do the rounds' and, coming upon the sleeping 'sentry', promptly shot him. He then discovered to his horror that he had shot his new son-in-law.

On being told the dreadful news, the grief-stricken young bride flung herself over the battlements and was killed. To complete this truly tragic tale, Colonel Warrender took his own life. Of this doomed trio only the bride – the 'White Lady' returns, so it is said, to haunt both fort and battlements.

Several serving officers can bear witness to the manifestation. During the early part of the nineteenth century the 'White Lady' was seen by a Major Black on the stairs leading up to the battlements. In 1880 two officers, a Captain Marvell Hull and a Lieutenant Hartland, came face to face with a pale and beautiful woman on a landing on the stairs. To the mutual consternation of both men, the woman vanished to all intents and purposes through a locked door. To add a romantic twist to the tale, it is said that the flowers that the young bride so desired were the blossoms from a wild white rose bush.

Apparitions do not always occur in human form, and from Kinvara, County Cork, come reports of one of Ireland's most common phenomena. Known as 'the black dog', it is found in all parts of the island. Lady Gregory, the well known nineteenth century 'lady of letters', described this manifestation in her celebrated work *Visions and Beliefs*. It was commonly seen as a monstrous black hound, the size of a calf, with red blazing eyes. In some of the traditional tales it is seen as a dog of ill omen, 'a messenger of death', but in others it is the guardian spirit of ancient tracks and sacred sites.

The reports in *Visions and Beliefs* conform to this basic description: 'As to the dog that used to be in the road, a friend of his was driving Father Boyle from Kinvara late one night and there it was first on one side of the road and then the other. At last he told Father Boyle and the priest said, "Look out for it now and you'll see it no more", and neither he did ...' Again, the familiar description turns up: '... and when he turned again there was something running through the field that was the size of a young calf and black, and it ran across the road and there were like the sounds of chains in it. When it came to that rock with the bush on it, it stopped and he could see a red light in its mouth ...'

Of course not all the apparitions that haunt Ireland's highways and byways are 'black dogs'. At Inchy, Gort, County Galway, a young farmer in the early part of this century heard what he took to be a herd of deer: '... and he heard something running from Inchy Weir, and he could see nothing, but the sound of its feet on the ground was like deer. And when it got to him, the dog got between him and the wall ...'

'Black dogs' are sometimes associated with bridges as 'guardians', but this was not the case with the bridge called 'the shying bridge' near Middleton, County Cork. The small bridge in question spans a narrow river about twelve miles or so from the town of Middleton. It is not a remarkable bridge in any respect, and as far as is known it has no historic connections. Yet it is said that horses in bygone days were loathe to cross it. The animals would exhibit great anxiety and rear and plunge out of control. By tradition, horses are regarded as being peculiarly sensitive to the paranormal.

One story associated with the 'shying bridge' is of a farmer who one Christmas was driving down to the bridge in a horse and trap to visit neighbours and deliver Christmas gifts. The farmer and his wife knew of the reputation of the bridge, but he made light of the idea that he would not be able to get his own docile mare over the bridge. 'Don't force her!,' warned his cowman. 'No good will come of it.'

When they got to the bridge, to the farmer's considerable annoyance the horse exhibited great fear and reared and backed away from it. The farmer fetched the animal several blows with the whip and, as a result, the horse bolted, turning the trap over and throwing the occupants over the low parapet into the waters of the icy river. The farmer's wife and one of their children were killed, and although the distraught farmer survived it is said he never again crossed the bridge, even on foot. Local tradition had it that a man who had been suicidal, owing to some mental disorder, had drowned himself in the river at that very spot, and that the body had been discovered trapped in the weeds below the bridge. It was his unhappy spirit that haunted the bridge and manifested itself to the horses, in order that others might 'keep him company' in death.

In the latter part of the last century, a large and fashionable house stood beside the main road into Bandon, County Cork. It was a little isolated from its neighbours by virtue of a long, sweeping drive that led up to the front door. One evening a female visitor was making her way up the drive to pay a courtesy call.

As she rounded the curve in the drive, she saw a gentleman approaching her, dressed all in black and wearing a tall silk hat. His head was bent, concealing his face, and she did not recognize him. As they came abreast, the man raised his head and looked straight at her. To the lady's horror, the face was so evil and repulsive that, instinctively, she recoiled against the shrubbery on the edge of the drive.

To her increased horror, the figure leant forward and touched her arm. Then, as she screamed for help, the figure vanished. It was said that the arm of the victim was paralysed for about two weeks, and the woman was found in a severe state of shock. When the unfortunate lady repeated her story, a number of people admitted that they also had encountered 'the man in the tall silk hat' but had not suffered quite such a close encounter. No one had any idea who the apparition represented.

It was common gossip in the area that the house was haunted, though by what or whom no one could say. While the name and exact location of the house is unclear, we do know that the lady's name was Hornibrook, and that she was in the employ of the Rev. H. Darling, the Rector of Kilpeacon, near Limerick.

Captain Dermot MacManus, the well known author and investigator into the paranormal, recounted in an article a very unusual event that happened in the early part of this century and was told to him in 1914. The location for the occurrence was Spike Island, Cobh, County Cork.

The episode concerned a little girl called Eileen who lived with her family on Spike Island, which lay across a narrow stretch of water from Cobh. Her father was in the army and was billeted on Spike Island. In the summertime the island was idyllic, and while there were few folk living on Spike, they were all neighbourly and pleasant. They included a doctor and his family and the residents of the military establishment where Eileen's father worked.

Eileen was in the habit of meeting the boat from the mainland daily, in order to collect her father's newspaper, and her way to the jetty took her past the doctor's house. The house was large and comfortable and surrounded by a five foot high wall that ran directly beside the road. To enliven her walk, Eileen would skip along beside the wall and occasionally jump up to catch at the branches. One day she suddenly looked up to see out of the corner of her eye 'something' looking over the wall. The 'thing' was roughly 'human' and very tall. It was grisly and slimy and, perhaps worst of all, where the thing's eyes should have been were only dark, cavernous holes.

To the little girl's horror, the thing began to move towards her. A voice inside Eileen's head warned her that 'if it looks at you, you will die'. This was the last straw, and the child turned and fled back up the road until she came to the first cottage, whereupon she fell in at the door and promptly collapsed. When she revived, she told the woman of the house what she had seen over the doctor's wall. To her surprise, the woman didn't seem too astounded at the revelation and said to Eileen, 'Others have seen that, alana!'

Many years later, when Eileen was fully grown, she returned to the island on a visit. By this time it had become the property of the Irish Army. Eileen was permitted to look round her old home and was escorted by a young lieutenant who, on having heard her tale, offered to tell her about 'his ghost' that he had seen up at the fort.

It seemed that one night a sentry had been reprimanded for firing a shot at 'a figure' he had seen coming out of one of the fort's outbuildings. The figure, so the sentry insisted, was of a large man in the old fashioned uniform of a British soldier. The loosing off of the shot was the reflex action of a very frightened man. Anxious to be fair about the event, the next night the young officer escorting Eileen had gone on duty with the sentry, and to his acute embarrassment there had been a second sighting of the apparition. This time it was the young officer himself who fired a shot in the direction of the figure. Both soldiers bore witness that the shot had been fired at virtually point blank range, but the figure still walked towards them, until suddenly vanishing. Curiously enough, so the lieutenant told Eileen, a few days after the incident the building from which the mysterious figure had emerged caught fire and was burned to the ground. The strange figure was never seen again.

Sometimes one is fortunate enough to come across an account of a paranormal event that is both gentle and appealing, with no sinister overtones, and which leaves the listener with a sense of awe and a conviction that 'love is stronger than death'. Such is the story of 'the girl in the yellow gown' that comes from Drimshallon in County Cork.

In the mid-eighteenth century in lovely Drimshallon Park, a Georgian house of some repute, lived Sir Patrick Duntarren and his wife and family. A young orphaned cousin, Anna Mary, lived with them. While a strong bond of affection existed between Sir Patrick and his young cousin, the same could not be said of the attitude of Lady Duntarren towards the girl. The older woman seemed jealous of Anna Mary, which mystified everyone. Anna Mary was a quiet, gentle soul who had endeared herself to the whole household with the exception of the spoiled and overbearing mistress of the house.

In the course of time, there arrived in the neighbourhood a famous portrait painter who was commissioned to paint the families of local dignitaries. Sir Patrick was delighted and promptly commissioned the artist to paint 'a conversation piece' of his family, in which he wished Anna Mary to take her place.

Lady Duntarren was furious at the suggestion and promptly forbade Anna Mary to intrude upon the portrait. Anna Mary was very naturally disappointed but insisted that she wished to cause no grief, and begged her cousin Patrick not to include her in the picture. The portrait was finished without her and shortly afterwards Anna Mary took up a position as a governess in Galway City, where she subsequently married a barrister, Tynan Driscoll. Her marriage was a happy and contented one and she died peacefully in Dublin in 1801.

In the summer of 1821, Anna Mary decided to revisit Drimshallon. Her cousin, Sir Patrick Duntarren, was now quite elderly. After the portrait was finished Sir Patrick had it hung in the morning room, and on one particular morning in 1821 Sir Patrick's manservant happened to glance at the picture. What he saw made him run to fetch his master.

Later, Sir Patrick told his sister what he had found upon arrival in the morning room. In the family portrait there stood beside the children a vision of a young girl in a pale yellow silk gown; the figure glowed and shimmered with light and its hands lay lightly on the shoulders of the little ones. Sir Patrick, with tears in his eyes, recognized his beloved Anna Mary. 'It is impossible to tell you,' Sir Patrick wrote in a letter, 'how lovely Anna Mary looked and how lovingly she touched the baby's hair … but the thing that impressed me most in this unusual occurrence was how properly Anna Mary fitted into the picture, just as I had always planned she should …

Subsequently over the years, Anna Mary was seen in the picture on several occasions. She was seen once or twice by a young invalid member of the family who said she felt 'a loving presence' and also said that she heard the rustle of a silken gown pass her, while the window onto the terrace opened and something like 'a shaft of light' passed through it. Anna Mary had come home.

3   The Monster of Glenade Lake

County Donegal is one of the wild and beautiful counties of the north of Ireland. This is the ancient land of Tyrconnell, famous for its small lakes, attractive glens and impressive and rugged coast. It is a county of pilgrimage too. On Lough Derg to the east of Donegal town is the small island known as St Patrick's Purgatory, a place much frequented by penitential pilgrims. The whole county has much of antiquarian interest as well as some of the most spectacular scenery in Ireland.

Glenade Lake, County Donegal, is the setting for the account of an event which is both unusual and thought provoking, dealing as it does with a non-human entity. The lake lies on the lefthand side of the main road from Bundoran, County Donegal, not far from Manorhamilton. It is the little graveyard of Conwel that has its part to play in the story; the Irish name 'Congbhail' means a 'church establishment' of some kind and must not be confused with the one outside Letterkenny. Both were ancient church sites, but it is in the first Conwel that a tombstone merits attention, as it bears an engraving of a strange beast with a spear in its neck.

The stone is said to commemorate a tragic incident in September, 1772, when a woman named Grace McLoughlin was washing her clothes at the lakeside. Suddenly a large animal emerged from the water, struck her down and began to devour her. Locally, the beast was known as a *dobharcu* (water otter) and it was feared by all the lakeside dwellers. Hearing the commotion, her husband rushed to her aid and managed to slay the beast with a pike or spear. Unfortunately, the dying screams of the monster attracted the attention of another monster in the lake who left the water and attacked the husband. The husband's brother Gilmartin arrived, but the two men could not cope with the infuriated beast and fled on horseback, pursued by the furious *dobharcu*. Finally the men barricaded themselves in an outhouse, placing the horses in the doorway. These wretched animals were fiercely savaged by the monster, but not before Gilmartin managed to spear the creature in the neck and kill it. Finally the two men returned to Glenade to recover the body of the unfortunate Mistress McLoughlin, who subsequently was interred in the graveyard of Conwel with the strange tombstone marking the spot.

Although written records of this grisly tale are hard to find, there is a very strong oral tradition of 'the monster', and the above account is similar to one found in the British Museum and in one or two local folk records, including a 1970 account in the *Leitrim Guardian*. Water demons or creatures with a kinship to the Scottish monster of Lough Ness are not uncommon in the history of the Irish faerie. Lough Neagh in County Antrim is also reported to have 'a creature', but by all accounts it is far less publicity conscious than the notorious 'Nessie'.

To return to the tradition of 'the messengers of death', one can examine an instance that is very different to either 'the black dog' or the 'black coach'. It falls more nearly into the realm of the 'bansidhe'. Purists may complain that non-human forms are not strictly 'bansidhe' for, by tradition, the 'bansidhe or fairy woman' takes the form of either a beautiful, red-haired girl (as is the case with the 'roe or red' bansidhes of Ulster) or the shape of an old hag of uncommonly unpleasant appearance, not unlike the 'y wrych-y griva' of Wales. Bansidhe come to warn of a death in certain chosen tribes or families. When they call, it is said that the one who is 'sent for' does not hear the cry but only those near them. One comes across varied reports of the bansidhe throughout the length and breadth of Ireland, even into the present day, and it is said that one never forgets hearing this cry. Traditionally, the bansidhe follows families whose surnames begin with a 'Mac' or an 'O', but in fact over seventy family names appear to qualify for this dubious honour. It may be, of course, that many of the names are linked by blood lines to the original family name.

The manifestation is not confined to Ireland. The Irish abroad may also be followed by the bansidhe, wherever they abide. It more generally cries or laments out of doors, although occasionally it is heard in the house, but mostly it sites itself beneath a window or beside a door. Most often it is seen, but sometimes only the 'cry' is heard, said to be anything from an eldritch shriek to a sobbing in Gaelic.

The incident of the Donegal bansidhe took place in an area known as 'the Rosses', on an estuary there. One of the points of interest is that what was thought to be a bansidhe did not assume traditional form, and therefore what one calls it is a matter of personal choice.

In the autumn of 1777 a minister of religion, Rev. James Crawford, was returning home from County Leitrim along the road to the Rosses with his sister-in-law riding pillion. Reaching the ford, he proceeded to cross it at the fording place, even though at one point the water lapped the saddle tips. Understandably, the lady became alarmed and cried out to Mr Crawford to turn back. Mr Crawford was reluctant to retrace his steps for, as he pointed out, it must be safe as he could see another rider crossing the ford ahead of them.

He called out to the rider, who turned in the saddle to reveal a face of such consummate evil that the clergyman turned back instantly, even though he was more than halfway across. His horse obviously agreed with him because, foaming at the mouth and with eyes rolling, the horse headed for the bank at speed.

Upon reaching home, the frightened pair related their experience to their families, who told Mr Crawford that not only was this phantom or bansidhe well known but, more unusually, there was more than one of them! There was in the area a strong belief that these were not ordinary phantoms, but that their mission was to warn certain people who were doomed to drown. They also were not averse to luring victims into the fateful ford by pretending to cross the ford safely. Thus their victims went to their death.

The irony of this cautionary tale is that, as a clergyman, James Crawford saw fit to ignore the timely warnings. Within a month, he once more essayed to cross the ford, and upon this occasion he was drowned. One wonders about the belief that a bansidhe, far from being a supernatural being, may be an apparition of the dead sent to warn or to lure others to their deaths. One also wonders if James Crawford's spirit joined 'the riders at the ford'.

A more familiar entity perhaps is the 'noisy, boisterous spirit', the poltergeist. This kind of manifestation is probably the most common of all in Ireland, and the incidents quoted in the annals of Irish paranormalism are very well documented and varied. There are numerous theories about the nature of this phenomenon, from the notion of 'little demons' on the perimeter of our world to the idea of a natural energy generated unconsciously by human beings themselves when they are in a state of instability, such as adolescents in that period of growth between childhood and adult life. It is one of the few paranormal manifestations that, by its physical behaviour, can cause actual bodily harm.

A slightly playful account of a poltergeist comes from the accounts of one of Ireland's most famous ghosthunters and writers, Sir Shane Leslie of Castle Leslie, Glaslough, County Monaghan. He tells of coming home from a pilgrimage in the company of two young Roman Catholic students. As the day was far spent when they arrived in a village that happened to be on his family land, they decided to go no farther but to put up for the night at the land agent's house. They were all tired and hoped to find somewhere to lay their weary heads.

Unfortunately this was not to be, at least not as far as Sir Shane's young companions were concerned, for some malicious entity spent the whole night removing the bed clothes and tossing the two young men about the bed all night. Next morning the red-eyed and weary travellers confided their plight, not to Sir Shane but to the landlord of the village pub where they had sought refuge, and he provided a novel if sectarian theory. He suggested that, seeing that they were of the 'Catholic persuasion', their tormentor had been the ghost of the former land agent, an unrelenting Protestant called James McCullough, who had taken 'a fit of the strunts' at having Catholic pilgrims making free with his bed!

On a more serious note, Sir Shane figured in another poltergeist case which is possibly the best known and certainly the best authenticated case in Irish poltergeist history. It happened in County Fermanagh at a place called Coonian. The location was a farm house, and the family living there was composed predominantly of young people – a common occurrence in the investigation of poltergeist phenomena. In the case of the Coonian ghost there were ample witnesses and a variety of clerical help. Indeed, the Catholic clergy were very helpful in providing information. One priest mentioned that in one of the beds he had seen 'a form under the blankets'.

Another took it upon himself to say Mass in the same bedroom, amid an atmosphere of great hostility that emanated from unseen forces in the room.

The variety of the phenomena was wide. It ranged from raps and knockings to whistling and bouts of singing. The children of the house were pinched and slapped or thrown out of bed and pelted with stones. The most harrowing manifestation took place in a small bedroom where witnesses encountered a form lying in bed, giving every indication of suffering what the Irish would describe as 'a hard death', with the agonies lasting up to ten minutes.

A number of the clergy who had ministered to the family suffered from all kinds of misfortune in forms of illness or nervous collapse. Certainly, there was much conjecture that the origins of the event were diabolical, and the centre of attention seemed to be the children. The neighbours could bear witness to numerous strange and unpleasant events that tried the family to the utmost. Finally, the family decided to emigrate to America, but it was rumoured that the entity manifested on the ship on which they travelled. Sir William Barret, the President of the London Society for Psychical Research and a well known Dublin physician, theorized that 'a radiant centre', as he called it, was present in one of the persons most closely involved who, quite unwittingly, provided a channel of energy. This case, which took place in the nineteenth century, excited a great deal of comment, and for those interested in this particular form of paranormalism it is fascinating to read the full account of the Coonian ghost.

The city of Dublin, the capital of the Republic of Ireland, in many respects overshadows the small county in which it is located, a county which once was divided into two parts known as Culann to the south and Fingal to the north. Later, these areas formed a substantial part of the Pale, after the coming of the Anglo-Norman lords. It was to their advantage to ring Dublin and its county with a barricade of stout castles. Many of the historic sites have a connection with these castles, which have produced, over the centuries, a wealth of paranormal information of varying kinds.

One such castle was Rathfarnham, built by Archbishop Adam Loftus in 1537. In the war of 1641 it became a place of siege, being at that time garrisoned by the forces of Parliament. After the battle of Rathmines in July 1649, it was eventually captured by Royalist forces and stubbornly held. Some two hundred years later, in more peaceful times, the castle was witness to a tragedy in the winter of 1840–1. It was common practice for the local inhabitants to skate on the castle pond, and on one such icy day a man with his dog, a curly-coated retriever, was disporting himself on the pond when the ice gave way and he was precipitated into the water.

Without hesitation the dog plunged in after his master, but both succumbed to the icy depths before help could reach them. So impressed were the villagers by the dog's heroism that a memorial was erected to commemorate the faithful retriever's actions. The apparition of the dog is alleged to haunt the castle grounds between the gate and Dodder Bridge, as many people have attested over the years. The apparition of the dog has company. The ghost of a little boy, murdered by tinkers, is also seen in the castle grounds from time to time.

Somewhat earlier in date, Tymon Castle was built in the thirteenth century by yet another Archbishop, Henry De Loundres of Dublin. The manor was granted to the Archbishop by King John in return for expenses incurred during the building of Dublin Castle. In later times the castle was demolished as it was in a dangerous condition.

Although the castle may have gone, the ghost of the castle remained and has been seen from time to time in or near where the castle stood. The apparition is said to be that of Olive Spencer, whose father was in possession of the castle at some earlier time. The story is, I suppose, familiar enough. Olive fell in love with a young steward, John Cremin, and of course her father vehemently disapproved. Casting about as to how he could get rid of Cremin, Olive's father managed to frame the young steward on a charge of theft. The young man, angry and distressed, went to see his employer to plead his innocence. In the heat of the moment an altercation broke out and Spencer fell down the stairs and broke his leg. John Cremin was arrested, accused of attempted murder and subsequently transported to Australia.

The griefstricken Olive locked herself in her chamber and committed suicide by taking poison. When the family retainers broke down the door, they found her lifeless body lying on the floor. Since that time the apparition of a young girl in a white ballgown has been seen in and around the ruins.

To complete a trilogy of haunted castles, one has but to go to Malahide Castle, founded in the twelfth century by Richard Talbot. It remained in the family down through the centuries until, in recent times, it passed into public ownership. Though much altered over the years, the great fifteenth century tower still stands, the Great Hall has its original walls and there are many fine furnishings, including a tryptych believed to have belonged to Mary Queen of Scots. To the east of the castle is the ruin of a chapel and the famous altar tomb of Maude Plunket. Her story, although not directly connected with the paranormal, is worth telling.

On the eve of Whitsun, 1329, Maude married the son of Lord Galtrim, yet before the day was out her husband, having been called out to deal with some renegades at Balbriggan, County Dublin, was tragically killed. The unhappy lady was thus, within the space of a single day, 'maid, wife and widow' – an event remembered in Gerald Griffen's ballad 'The Bride of Malahide'. Maude did marry again and became wife to Lord Talbot, Admiral of Malahide and Seas Adjoining.

Malahide is, beyond doubt, a dwelling of much distinction. The previously mentioned Flemish tryptych, known as 'The Coronation of the Virgin', depicts four angels proceeding to place a crown on Our Lady's head. There is a mysterious tale attached to this work of art. The Talbot family were dispossessed during the Cromwellian period and a man called Miles Corbet, Chief Baron of Ireland, took up residence at Malahide. Corbet was one of the regicides who signed the death warrant of Charles I and was consequently regarded as a particularly odious creature. It was said that Corbet was a deeply unhappy man, plagued by a guilty conscience that allowed little sleep or content. He rode about the estate after dark on a great white horse called 'Pooka'. It was a rather ominous name, insofar as it was the name of a fairy being, and the locals saw no good coming of it. Indeed the Corbet fortunes steadily declined until, along with the other regicides, 'the hue and cry' went out for him on the orders of Charles II at the time of the Restoration. Corbet fled to Delft in Holland but was captured and brought to London, where he was executed – an event recorded by Samuel Pepys on 19 April 1662.

But to return to the tale attached to the tryptych: while Corbet was in residence, this venerated object mysteriously disappeared from its place and the wall remained blank for twelve years. Many believed that Our Lady had 'spirited it away'. The moment that Corbet's head was on the block, the tryptych miraculously was restored to its rightful place. Those of a more pragmatic disposition, when questioned about the mysterious disappearance of the tryptych, were inclined towards the possibility that some human agency had seen fit to spirit it away until 'the King enjoyed his own again'.

At the far end of the Great Hall can be found a very small door of Alice-in-Wonderland proportions. It is called Puck's staircase and was said to originally have led to the quarters of a tiny man, no more than four foot tall. He was associated with the castle from medieval times and had been a faithful retainer to his lord, although life for him in those brutal days was far from easy. Sadly, in the end he had taken his own life. When Lord Talbot's death broke the family connection with the castle after nearly 800 years, 'Puck' reappeared in his place as 'guardian' of the castle he had served so faithfully. Some say that he can still be seen; indeed, family members are said to have seen him from the eighteenth century right up until the 1970s.

In a place so steeped in history it would be expected that there would be 'inhabitants' in the castle that might manifest from time to time. Puck is certainly not the only ghost of Malahide. It also boasts of a 'White Lady' said to manifest in the Great Hall. Little is known of this charming vision except that the portrait of a lady in a white gown that hangs in the castle is said to be her. Apparently she is able, on occasion, to become solid and three-dimensional, and she can step out from her gilded frame to roam the castle at will. It is surprising that the tragic Maude Plunket, the young woman who was 'maid, wife and widow' between one sunrise and sunset, does not make her presence known, but there is no evidence at all that her sorrowful shade walks in Malahide's halls.

Near Monkstown, County Dublin, another widow is said to walk a certain hill nearby, known as Widow Gammon's Hill. The story goes that she was responsible for the betrayal of a group of religious that hid from Cromwellian troops in the area. Because of the widow's action, the group were arrested and executed. As a result of this treacherous deed, the widow was doomed to walk the hill as a penance.

Local people are said to have seen the apparition both on the hill and in a local graveyard where she was seen wandering although the gates were locked. Another witness saw her coming out of the castle ruins and again she held in one hand, as she had done in the graveyard, a large key, while in the other she held what looked like an axe. On a later occasion the apparition was seen coming from the ruins, then heading for the graveyard and passing through the locked gates. As one may readily understand, local folk are not anxious to pass Widow Gammon's Hill after dark.

Over the years as a researcher I have been fortunate enough to obtain help and information from a large cross-section of the general public, as well as friends and colleagues. Many of the personal stories I have heard were very moving: some spoke of the hope for an existence beyond the grave, some told simply and factually of encounters with phenomena from other times that had existed down through the centuries and manifested to witnesses of every century. Every piece of information in its own way contributed something of value, even when the witnesses would declare a little self-consciously that they 'didn't believe in those kinds of things'. Yet despite misgivings, these witnesses had seen fit to confide in someone who they hoped might understand.

In August of 1983 I received a letter from a Mr Campbell of Dublin who wrote concerning certain information he had on the bansidhe. He wrote that when he was about ten years old, some fifty years earlier, he had been walking along a road in Westmeath on a dreary winter evening when, to his horror, he heard a 'sharp, shrill outcry' that was both weird and terrible. He took to his heels and never drew breath until he was safe in his grandmother's house in the village of Killucan. A death followed this incident. Two years later the same boy witnessed a large glass picture frame falling to the ground in his grandmother's house, without any tangible reason why it should have come off the wall. Three days after this event his uncle was killed in an accident in a hayfield, an incident that the boy witnessed. Mr Campbell suggested that the noise he had heard on the first occasion in the road was the cry of the bansidhe. He also said that on several occasions he appeared to exercise a measure of ESP (extrasensory perception), for he heard rapping and knockings. And he discovered a gift for water divining which both pleased and surprised him.

A correspondent from Dun Laoihaire also experienced the 'falling picture' syndrome and heard alarming 'knockings' in the middle of the night in August, 1955. He rose from his bed and went to the front door where the knocks seemed to come from, but there was no one there. In the house his two children were sound asleep, as was the dog. So Mr R. R. went back to bed. The next night the same thing happened again, only this time when he went to the door he found a taxi driver he knew well, who told him that he had been sent to take him to the hospital where Mr R. R's wife was gravely ill. A few hours later she died while her husband was at the bedside.

The witness was utterly convinced that the 'knocking' had some connection with subsequent events, although he had never before had any kind of paranormal experience. He did, however, have a very open and informed mind on psychic matters. Every year similar cases occur and are reported on by responsible people. One correspondent told me of death knocks that were heard in a Belfast house only days before a member of the family was drowned in Buenos Aires. Even more strange, a second bout of knocks occurred a year later and a tragically similar accident came about with the drowning of another member of the family off Donaghadee, County Down. The witness said that she would never forget the eerie, cavernous 'knocks' that she knew without being told were the herald of some dreadful news. In the cases of those who have heard the bansidhe quite often, witnesses will say that they recognized the cry even though they had never heard it before. One can only wonder if part of the bansidhe phenomenon is an inherited memory within ourselves that lies dormant until the appointed time comes for it to be heard.

In Lucan, County Dublin, a report was received from a Mr Farrel about an incident which happened in 1971. A newly married man at the time, Mr Farrel had bought a house on the north side of Dublin and was in the house one morning at about 2.30 a.m. when he woke to a terrifying sight. He described how, hovering above the bed, was a 'gaseous object' about the size of an adult person but with no face or hair. It was greyish in colour. At that moment his wife woke also and saw the object and was deeply disturbed. Eventually the object moved away until it finally vanished altogether.

Needless to say, the young couple had received such a severe fright that they debated as to whether they should leave the house and move away. However, they worried that perhaps *they* were haunted and not the house, in which case moving house would be of little avail. In the end, good sense prevailed and they stayed put for another five years with no 'repeat performance'.

As Mr Farrel rightly pointed out, had he alone seen the object he might have dismissed it as a nightmare, but when his wife described the object exactly as he too saw it the fact that they could be sharing a nightmare or hallucination seemed unlikely. He pointed out that the blinds were drawn and the room was very dark. They experimented with opening and shutting the blinds and switching on and off various lights; they even examined the street lighting but they could not produce a comparable effect. The most frightening aspect of the whole episode was that while the object was manifesting it was quite literally hovering only inches above their heads.

I did suggest to Mr Farrel that he might have been the percipient of the experience and transmitted the vision telepathically to his wife as she lay beside him, but it was a possibility we could not test. Upon reflection, after having come across one or two cases of two people perceiving the same thing, one does wonder what effect such an experience could have on 'down-to-earth' people who have no interest in or contact with paranormal events. Yet similar experiences are told throughout history and, regardless of time and place, bear a close resemblance in the telling.

It was to ordinary people that the frightening events of the Hell Fire Club and Killakee House outside of Rathfarnham occurred, and the only consoling thought is that seldom are events as horrendous as these. The so-called Hell Fire Club stands about four miles from Rathfarnham and was built by Mr Speaker Connolly, the Speaker of the Irish House of Commons, in 1720 as a shooting lodge. It was said that the foundation stones came from an ancient cairn in the area. In 1735 Richard Parsons, first Earl of Ross, and his companion, the artist James Worsdale, bought the building and installed the group that made up the membership of the Hell Fire Club. It was modelled on the notorious English version, whose chief interest was occult practice and extreme debauchery.

Local inhabitants were terrified at the nightly happenings at the club; there were sounds of screams and animal-like roarings, and this was accompanied by reports of victims forced to take part in all kinds of obscene rituals. People believe that the Devil himself manifested at the club and that murdered victims haunted the spot. While it was in use, most God-fearing people shunned it and its occupants, but in later times, in the 1960s, there was renewed activity from a contemporary coven of witches which reawakened old fears. The coven was said to contain a number of well-known and indeed important people, and it was common belief that to betray the secrets of the coven was to court disaster and death.

The reputation of the Hell Fire Club was to be matched by a house not far distant, Killakee House. This house was noted for the fact that, among other things, it was haunted by a monstrous cat. It was thought that the apparition was that of a cat which had been used in the occult practices at the club and had subsequently met its death by being dowsed in spirit and set on fire by members of the coven. The cat was seen by numerous witnesses both around the house and grounds and was described as 'black and as large as an Airedale dog'. Eventually, an artist who encountered it captured it on canvas, and in the 1960s the portrait hung in the hall of the house.

Another apparition associated with the house was that of a crippled boy who almost always accompanied the cat, and this was said to be the spirit of a crippled child who had been incarcerated and murdered in the house. He was believed to have been buried somewhere in the vicinity of the house itself. The two apparitions seen together constituted a terrifying sight. Other daytime apparitions seen by witnesses included two nuns and a 'Spanish looking man' who manifested in the courtyard.

An upstairs room and corridor was haunted by a man in a bloodstained shirt, his clothes reminiscent of the 1920s and believed to be connected with 'the Troubles'. In the corridor the sound of running feet was often heard and the noises culminated in a bedroom where it is thought the man was shot down. The house was occupied by a family who ran an Art Centre and workshops at this time, and they were deeply troubled by all kinds of poltergeist activity which included changes of temperature, various noises and the sound of tinkling bells. Items of furniture were smashed up until the remains were literally matchwood and mysterious 'apports' were transported into the house in the shape of all kinds of headwear, from babies' bonnets to men's caps. Coins and milk-bottle tops also were scattered about. It would be no exaggeration to say that the people in the house were subject to a continuing assault both by night and day; in addition, they suffered various minor accidents and one member of the family was pushed down the stairs. It was a place that reeked of fear and unseen malevolent presences. The ministrations of the church seemed to have little or no effect and a number of paranormalists, including myself, can bear witness to the unpleasantness of the place. A subsequent family moved in after the house lay empty for a while and, surprisingly, they appeared to suffer no harassment.

Ireland's Eye is a small wedge-shaped mass of quartzite north of Howth, County Dublin, which forms a natural breakwater to Howth Harbour. The small church of Saint Nessan was built here on the site of an older seventh century building. The church possessed a copy of the Four Gospels dating from the seventh century, which is now in the library of Trinity College, Dublin. The island had some value as a tourist site and sometimes the over curious visitor would miss the boat back, forcing him to spend longer than he might have wished on the island.

Over fifty years ago a pair of young lovers found themselves in this predicament and had to settle for spending the night on Ireland's Eye. Sheltering out of the wind, they made themselves as comfortable as they could, confident that at daybreak they would be taken off the island by local fishermen. They were rescued, of course, but they had a strange tale to tell the next day.

The girl insisted that during the night she heard two voices, those of a man and a woman, raised in a very acrimonious argument. A few moments later the young man saw illuminated in a hazy light the figure of an older man walking along the shoreline. Thinking that the man was another marooned tourist, he shouted to him, but to the young man's consternation the figure vanished. On a different occasion two fishermen rowing just off shore also saw an elderly man on the shore, but as the witnesses 'Hallooed' the figure vanished into a hazy mist.

Local people say that in the 1850s a man called Kirwan murdered his wife on the island. The couple had asked to be rowed out to the island and then to be picked up again at a particular time and returned to the mainland. When the boatman returned to the island to fetch them, he found only Mr Kirwan awaiting him. He told the boatman that his wife had wanted to go swimming and that she had not returned to the designated meeting place. A search party was raised and they found Mrs Kirwan's body, clad in a bathing dress, at a spot known as 'the Long Hole'. The verdict recorded was 'death by drowning'. An uneasy quiet lay over the incident, and a month or so after the supposed accident in October, 1852, an order was signed for the exhumation of the body. A further examination showed that the woman had been strangled.

After what seemed an indecently short time as a widower, Kirwan had remarried, and this unseemly haste had provoked much comment among his neighbours. It was hardly surprising, then, when Kirwan was arrested and brought in for questioning. In due course he was tried and sentenced to death, but because of a weakness in the case for the prosecution the sentence was commuted and Kirwan reprieved to serve a prison sentence.

Nearly fifteen years later, on a summer evening in 1867, a boatman was asked to take a stranger, a man dressed in black, out to Ireland's Eye. The stranger was elderly and said little on the trip. When he got to the island he walked in the direction of where the body of the woman had been found those many years ago. He stood for a long moment staring at the spot and then walked swiftly back to the boat, and indicated to the boatman that he wished to be returned to the mainland. Later the boatman told his friends that he knew it was Kirwan, for he recognized him despite the age difference. The stranger in black was not seen again.

One may end this chapter, as it was begun, with stories of dogs. One such story concerns the well known Saint Patrick's Cathedral in Dublin, which once had Jonathan Swift as its Dean. A monument within its precincts tells the tale of Captain John McNeill Boyd and his dog. The captain was drowned at Dun Laoghaire in 1861.

On the night of 8 February 1861 a severe gale blew up in the Irish Sea and raged all night. By dawn the entry to Dun

Laoghaire harbour was blocked by massive amounts of debris from shattered vessels, as well as the bodies of those killed at sea by the raging wind and weather. It was essential to clear the harbourways to assist partially disabled vessels to get into port. The man designated to organize these vital rescue operations was Captain McNeill Boyd, with the crew of the coastguard vessel the Ajax.

One particular problem presented great difficulty: Three large coal-boats had jammed together in the harbour entry; they were smashed and being constantly ground against the rocks. Wounded and half-drowned sailors clung to these battered ships. Captain Boyd and his crew, heedless of their own lives, scrambled to save who they could. Then, with a terrifying roar, a huge wave crashed down on to the Ajax and her crew were swept into the raging seas, Captain Boyd among them.

At first they could not find the Captain's body; then, several days after the storm abated, the body was discovered and brought to shore. On the day of the funeral, Dublin came to a standstill to accommodate the great press of people who had travelled from near and far to honour the courage of John McNeill Boyd and his crew in their attempt to save the lives of the colliers. Directly behind the hearse one mourner stood out in particular, a large black Newfoundland dog. He was Captain John's dog Alex who had gone everywhere with his master before that fatal night. He lay silently beside the bier in the cathedral, then he rose and followed the other mourners to the graveside. When the earth had been placed on the coffin the dog mounted the soil and lay, head on paws, to watch with his master. For a week or more the dog refused all friendly ministrations and care, refusing to leave Captain John. Finally the heartbroken creature followed his master through the waters of death.

This tragic sequel so moved the citizens of Dublin that, when a memorial was raised to Captain McNeill Boyd in the cathedral, they also remembered Alex. But that is not quite the end of the story. In the years that followed, visitors to evensong would sometimes see, in the shadows, a large black dog sitting quietly on the steps of Captain John's memorial. The last time that the faithful Alex was seen is believed to have been in the late 1950s, when he was observed by a member of the cathedral clergy. Perhaps there should be inscribed on such a memorial stone two simple words: 'semper fidelis'.

Another of the famous 'black dogs' was to be seen in a town setting, in contrast to the more common country setting. There were many reports of a 'black dog' on the banks of the Grand Canal in Dublin. This was a beast of a very fierce disposition who chose as his beat the stretch of bank between the Rialto Bridge and the Inchicore Bridge.

In 1971 a student going home alone late one night saw a very large and solid shape loping towards him. While it was obviously not uncommon to meet a stray dog, it was the size of the creature that caused the boy some consternation. 'It was as tall as a calf and somehow the eyes were yellow and smouldering, like as though they were lit from inside by flames. It seemed to be making straight for me, as though it had come especially to meet me,' the student explained. 'I was never as frightened in my life and I stood stock still and my mouth was that dry, I couldn't utter a sound. So I blessed myself and it still came on, so then I cried out the name of the Blessed Trinity and blessed myself again. As God is my witness, the beast leapt into the air and jumped into the water, I could still see its blazing eyes. Then it was gone and I saw it no more.' Over twenty years later, that same man, now a very respected member of the legal fraternity, can still recall his encounter with 'the black dog' as though it were only yesterday!

4 The Boy at the Window

The county of Galway possesses two contrasting features, the flat and fertile eastern plain running northwards eventually to the Roscommon border, and the mountainous, northwestern half that extends from Galway Bay to the waters of Killary Harbour. It includes the beautiful Lough Corrib and the attractive region of Connemara; for literary folk, of course, it contains what is known as 'Joyce's Country', after Ireland's famous son James Joyce. It has a rugged Atlantic coastline, while in Galway Bay itself are the well known Aran islands. Galway owes its culture to Spanish influences and blood as much as to its native peoples, as many survivors of Philip of Spain's ill-fated Armada found their way here. It is a county steeped in turbulent history and breathtaking beauty.

Apart from the James Joyce tradition, it was to Galway that W.B. Yeats came for rest and rehabilitation in his busy life. He and his family took up residence in Ballylee Castle or Yeats' Tower, as it came to be called, at Thoor, Ballylee, County Galway. The tower was first mentioned in the Book of Connaught in 1585. It is a square, gaunt building with a huddle of outbuildings at its feet, and a mill and a bridge. Nowadays it is a place of pilgrimage for all those lovers of Yeats' poetry, and here we can find 'the winding stair', one of the poet's dearest themes. It has to be said that the restoration of this medieval tower was a labour of love for Yeats, and he and his family lived there between 1921 and 1928. In 1948 the Abbey Theatre, Dublin, placed an inscription on the Tower to honour their great companion in art.

> I, the poet William Yeats
> With old mill boards and sea green slates
> And smithy work from the Gort forge

Restored this tower for my wife George
And may these characters remain
When all is ruin once again.

Hopefully, that will be a long time in coming, as the tower is now in the professional and loving care of the Western Region Tourist authorities. Now many visitors may see 'the holy ground' for themselves.

One such visitor was David Blinkthorne who, in the summer of 1989, set out with his family from England on a touring holiday around County Galway. One of the 'musts' on their tour was Thoor, Ballylee. They arrived about fifteen minutes before the premises closed for the day, too late for the conducted tour of the tower. However, seeing how interested Mr Blinkthorne was in taking one or two photographs, the custodian agreed to allow him a hasty tour of the place. One photograph that he particularly wanted was of Yeats' sitting-room, and the curator agreed to unfold the shutters again to enable the picture to be taken. The shutters were unbarred and the photographer left alone to take his shot while his family enjoyed the view from the top of the tower. It was, in fact, the work of but a moment. There was very little furniture in the room, save for a chair or two: just the bare wooden floor and a door that led out onto the winding stair that led eventually to the tower top. For those who may be interested, the camera used was a Practica containing a Kodak film (400 ASA). No flash was used.

When Mr Blinkthorne returned home the negatives were developed and, to his surprise, the image appearing on one photograph bore no resemblance to anything else contained on the roll of film. The shot of the sitting-room in the tower showed an open window with the sun streaming in. The window is plainly delineated, as is one wall with a framed picture on it, and a chair standing beside the window shows up clear and sharp. In the foreground is a dark silhouette of a 'boy' whose head reaches just above the windowsill and appears to be bisected by it. There is a strong outline of the figure to mid-calf; his hair appears to be short, his ears stick out and his hands are in the pockets of what may be dungarees. Some people who have examined the photo say that the boy is looking towards the camera; others say that he is facing the window and that little straps or braces can be seen on the garment he is wearing. He is standing oddly, too, knees close together and at an angle to the rest of the photograph – or so it seems.

All the other photos on the roll were 'normal' and there were no flaws on any of them, just as there was no little boy present in the room when Mr Blinkthorne took the photograph, his own son being at the top of the tower with his mother. One other thing is obvious: portions of the chair actually appear to protrude through the apparitional body.

As a result of this photograph, a brief investigation was carried out at the tower, both by a professional photographer and a paranormal researcher. The photographer had experimented with trying to reproduce the effect seen on the photo, and after a number of lengthy and futile attempts she said she could think of no method by which the same effect with light, stance and density of silhouette could be achieved. A second set of photos were taken by a third party, and again nothing resulted.

The paranormalist examined the room and questioned members of staff but there was little information to add, save that W. B. Yeats himself had believed that the tower had been haunted by an Anglo-Norman soldier who he once had seen on the stair. An earlier curator also had believed the tower haunted and had been reluctant to go up the stairs as the day turned to evening. Her feeling was shared by a resident small dog who exhibited some unease in the downstairs room.

So, who was the boy in the window? Is he perhaps some earlier echo of those who had lived there? Yeats' own child perhaps, or do we have the gender wrong? Could it be some aetheric record of the little boy who, at the precise time that his father was taking the photo, somehow imprinted on the shot, despite the fact that he was in another part of the tower? The truth is that we have no idea how the photograph came about. It seems very unlikely that it was a carefully planned hoax, bearing in mind the lack of time for preparation to perpetrate such an event. We shall never know, I suspect, how the 'boy at Ballylee' imprinted himself on the shadows at Thoor.

Kinvarra stands at the head of Kinvarra Bay, County Galway, and here too the 'An caoiste bodhar' or black coach has been seen, but it is a coach with a difference. It ran on the Kinvarra road and was variously described as a 'coach' or 'carriage'.

Witnesses would draw off the road to let it pass, and as it passed one was said to be able to see that the four horses were headless and the two men sitting on the box were headless too.

At nearby Loughrea, a man standing at the corner of a pond saw the coach at the corner, and while he noted the headless horses he also noted that the coach appeared to be full of children dressed in white. A nineteenth century witness, a Mrs Ann Madden, told how in the night she had woken and heard 'a car' rattling by. Upon enquiry from her neighbours in the morning she was told that 'the coach with the headless ones' had passed and there would be misfortune following.

Another woman, a Mrs Casey, told how a young lad of her acquaintance had seen the coach, but the event was somewhat more exotic. There were people in the coach, ladies with flowers in their hair, and in this instance there was a strong suggestion that this was not the black coach but a 'fairy coach' complete with the fairy host who had attempted to lure a man on the road in to going with them. This coach seemed to travel the roads around 11.00 p.m. There was a companion coach on the Kilcolgan/Oranmore road which possessed grand ladies and flowers, too, although to look on this coach, so the witness stated, was to incur blindness.

These 'coaches' appear to fall into three categories. One is a 'death or black coach' which, as in the case of a bansidhe, may follow a certain clan or family or may foretell disaster in general. Another is the 'fairy coach' which has lights and fairy folk aboard and may be used to lure humans to their revels. A third kind are the apparitional coaches which have some connection to a specific event.

A typical example is the Antrim Castle Coach which plunged into the Long Pond at the Castle on May Eve after a drunken coachman lost his way, and all on board were killed. This coach is said to come hurtling down the Long Pond on May Eve and disappear under the water. Yet while this phenomenon is quite common in Irish contexts, it is also to be found throughout Great Britain in similar forms.

Yet another incident concerning the poet William Butler Yeats is told around the area of Renvyle in Connemara. This picturesque part of the coast is famed for its wide and sandy beaches and panoramic views. Significant parts of Ireland's stormy past too are recollected in the area. There is Renvyle

Castle, held by the Boyces and the O Flahertys while the great
Queen Maeve stormed the castle in vain. Then there are older
relics such as a dolmen, a ruin of an ancient church and a holy
well, one of three thousand once said to exist in Ireland. This
too was one of the last districts where 'the keening' was heard,
the eerie cry of women mourning a death. Now the modern
world has caught up with Renvyle and Renvyle House became a
luxury hotel.

The house was built by Sir Edward Lutyens about 1932 and
was originally owned by the Gogarty family, among whose
famous sons was St John Gogarty, poet and friend of James
Joyce. It is said that he was the original 'Buck Mulligan' in James
Joyce's *Ulysses*. The original Gogarty house was burnt down in
the 'Troubles'. After 1922 Gogarty rebuilt the house and it
became the gathering place for the famous writers of the day,
including Ireland's rising star, W. B. Yeats.

Interspersed with a profound interest in literature was a
growing absorption in the occult and the paranormal among the
intellectuals, of which two of the foremost were Yeats and
Gogarty. Renvyle therefore became a popular place for
paranormal experiments. Many seances were held in the house
and it became common knowledge that the house acquired
something of an 'atmosphere'. There were a number of
incidents quoted and several visitors admitted to witnessing
paranormal events, mostly unspecified. In particular, there was
one room where the guests complained that they felt 'someone'
was in the room with them. One witness saw a man looking over
her shoulder into the dressing table mirror.

Subsequently the hotel management called in a priest to say
Mass in the house, a practice which continued as late as 1955.
During this time the haunted room was occupied by the hotel
manager and his father, who was not particularly susceptible to
talk of 'the paranormal'. During the night the manager was
continually disturbed by a loud 'clicking' sound, while his father
slumbered peacefully. The manager knew that it was assumed
that the room was the one used by Yeats and others to conduct
seances. It was in this room that the figure appeared in the
mirror, and the witness told of 'a tall man wearing a dark suit'.
The figure bore a strong resemblance to Yeats himself.

By 1966 interest had grown in the haunting of Renvyle
House. There had been several reports by staff and guests, and

one of the maids had seen a male figure materialize in a corridor then vanish into thin air. This happened not once but several times. A private seance was held in the room, conducted by the well known American paranormalist Hans Holzer and others. The second floor room was examined minutely.

Several interesting things came to light, including the fact that the date '1928' appeared significant and the distinct impression that the 'presence' was both rude and unpleasant. The medium also picked up images of 'men in long dresses' and feelings of fire and death in the room, although the images seemed to represent different times in the history of the house. The 'vanishing man' in the corridor was also said to be tall and dressed in a dark suit, and another visitor confirmed the maid's story in 1966. Inevitably the connection with W. B. Yeats was made.

The fact was also revealed that there had been two houses built at Renvyle, one on the ruins of the other, with the seances having taken place in the house that had existed before the fire. To these reports was added another, that of the manifestation of a boy in a brown velvet suit, aged about twelve. It seemed that this tragic child had taken his own life by hanging and communicated this information to Yeats by means of automatic writing. To add a bizarre twist, Yeats is supposed to have set down certain 'house rules' for the entity as to what he might or might not do in case he 'frightened the children'. Some measure of rapport was reached and the entity revealed his name, Harold Blake, and the circumstances of his death. Mrs Yeats, who had mediumistic ability, saw the child materialize in the original haunted room and found that the 'uneasy feelings' that the original seances had uncovered had taken place in the approximate area where the old house had stood, while the actual sensations experienced by the medium took place in the area of the rebuilt house, restored after the fire.

Were there other ghosts at Renvyle, besides the 'tall dark man' and the 'suicide'? Could it be that Yeats, having been conscious in his own lifetime of the tragic suicide, continued in the afterlife to attempt to encourage investigators who came after him to contact both the discarnate personalities of 'dark man and boy'? I suppose that it is a possibility, perhaps as much a possibility as that Yeats and the 'dark man' were one and the same.

*   *   *

There are, from time to time, reports of what may be termed 'anniversary ghosts' – that is, apparitions or other paranormal manifestations that take place on a regular date, connected to some unfortunate happening of an earlier time. Both in Ireland and the rest of Britain there are many witness reports on this particular kind of event. Many are attached to battlefields and similar affrays. In England, the Battle of Edgehill was a case in point, where it is said the battle was refought over a number of years in the skies over the original field. Not only were apparitions of fighting men seen, but the noise of guns and the shouts of battle created such a din that birds were known to leave their roosts and cattle panicked in the fields.

In Ireland, one of the best known examples of this phenomenon was said to take place at Dun An Òir, County Kerry. In October, 1589, during the Desmond rebellion, a force of 800 Spaniards landed on the Dingle Peninsula to assist the rebels. Getting little or no help from the local Irish, they were besieged by English troops under Lord Grey de Wilton and forced to surrender. To de Wilton's great dishonour, they were almost immediately butchered, the number of the slain being put at 600 unarmed men. It is said that on the anniversary of the massacre, the screams of the dying Spaniards can be heard and some witnesses have spoken of seeing 'ghastly figures' that gave off a dreadful stench of decay.

In County Kildare, at Clongowes Wood, Clane, another apparition was seen, not on a regular basis but once and once only.

The house at Clongowes had been the home of the Wogan-Browne family since 1667. Then, in the early part of the nineteenth century, General Michael Wogan-Browne sold off the estate to a religious order. Up until the nineteenth century, the house had been home to distinguished military families. Later, when the house became an exclusive boys' school, one of its pupils had been the author James Joyce.

General Michael Wogan-Browne had served as an aide to the King of Saxony, and later another member of the family became a serving Marshal in the Austrian army. One afternoon in the early 1800s, the two young sisters of the Marshal serving in Austria were on their way home across the park to the house as the day closed in. As they came into the warmth and light of the great hall they saw, standing at the foot of the stairs leading to the upper apartments, the figure of a young man dressed in military uniform. The girls stared in paralysed horror at the man's ashen face; it was bloody and pain-wracked. His clothes, too, were dirty and bloodstained.

As they watched, the figure moved up the stairs and eventually disappeared through one of the doors leading out of the upper gallery into the bedchamber of their missing brother. For a long moment the two women did not move. Then they hurried to acquaint their parents with what they had seen. More dreadfully, they revealed that they had recognized the form and features of their brother. Gradually the family came to the conclusion that the event had only one interpretation: the young man had perished in battle. So convinced were they that Mass was said and a wake held for the departed son of the house.

News from the far off European battle front was very sparse, and so it was several weeks before they received confirmation that Marshal Wogan-Browne had indeed been killed in battle at Prague. He had, the message told them, shown courage well in excess of his duty and had been instrumental in saving many of his comrades from the fate that he himself had suffered. It further transpired that it had been on the selfsame day that his sisters had seen the apparition that Wogan-Browne had perished. The soldier as he lay dying, one supposes, had loving thoughts of home and family, and his brave spirit had returned to familiar surroundings. As a separate point of interest, Clongowes Wood was also said to possess 'a black dog' seen from time to time in the house.

Another story with a European background comes from County Leitrim, at a place named Drumshambo. The haunting of Drumshambo began with the marriage in 1873 of the daughter of the house to a Polish cavalry officer, Count Alexander Sczriny. The young countess was soon to discover that, along with wealth and title, she had also inherited a legend and a curse, known as 'the Weeping Wall'. There is a strong tradition of 'cursing' in Ireland, by which the innocent victim of some dark deed may seek redress through the supernatural justice of a higher being. The two curses most to be feared were the curse of the priest and the mother's or widow's curse. One did not utter a curse without due consideration, for if it was unjustified the ill fortune would rebound on the head of the curser. Formal cursing took place in public, and in the case of a woman she would have knelt down in the street and unbound her hair before voicing her complaint. The Sczriny curse had been uttered for a familiar and tragic reason.

A century before the marriage of the Drumshambo heiress, the then heir to the Sczriny title had paid with his life on a hangman's rope for the rape of a village girl in Poland. The girl's mother, mourning for her daughter, had uttered a terrible curse as the execution was carried out. 'No Sczriny will find peace,' she cried. 'Misfortune will follow every bearer of that name! But I say this: Before disaster strikes, the Sczriny will be warned. Let them escape, if they can!'

And so the curse took effect. In each generation tragedy overtook the next heir, and a dreadful warning was enacted. While it was seen several times in Poland, it was a hundred years before it manifested itself in Ireland, at Drumshambo. In the summer of 1888, the Countess Moira and her husband decided to take their two children − Peter, aged fourteen and Maria, aged ten − home to Drumshambo to visit their grandparents. The children had only been to Drumshambo once or twice before, so they all looked forward to a very happy reunion.

The summer sped by and all too soon the count said regretfully that they had to return home, via Paris, where he had business to transact. Within twenty-four hours, a bout of very stormy weather blew up and even the seasoned timbers of Drumshambo shuddered in the onslaught. The count had been suffering from a mild chill, and so as to gather his strength for the journey ahead he took to his bed for a day or two. The evening before the journey, the count again went to bed early, leaving his children, wife and her parents in the library. Suddenly young Peter grabbed his mother's arm. 'Look Mother! Look at the wall!' Everyone fell silent as they saw the transformation taking place on the wall at the far end of the room. First the wall seemed to darken, then large drops of slimy moisture oozed from the paper onto the floor. The room grew very cold, and finally an invisible hand traced the name 'Alexander' onto the wall.

At the sight of her husband's name, the Countess Moira grew deathly pale and, springing to her feet, fled upstairs to where her husband lay sleeping. Her young son fled after her, but took a shorter route to his father's room. As he reached the bedroom door ahead of his mother a tremendous gust of wind shook the whole house. There was a ghastly sound of rending timbers and the entire place seemed as if it might fall about them. Young Peter flung himself bodily at the bedroom door, and as it flew open he saw the massive chimney piece crash down on the bed where Count Alexander lay, killing him instantly.

The sequel to this tragedy was revealed in a few days. A letter arrived from Poland in which the count's mother explained that she had been sitting alone in her own salon when she, too, saw her son's name traced on the wall. The tragic lady had seen it all before, at the death of her other son, Stefan, who had been savaged by a horse. This time, as the wall dripped and oozed, the lady noted that the clock on the wall showed the time to be nine minutes past ten. In Drumshambo, the wall 'wept' at ten o'clock.

This was not the last to be heard of the 'weeping wall'. In 1940 the wall wept again for Casimir, Alexander's great-grandson, killed in a plane crash, and again for another Sczriny killed during the Second World War in 1943. In this last instance, the circumstances were not clearly known. Nor do we know if the wall has 'wept' for the last time.

5   The Fighting Men of Limerick

Few people need reminding that the history of Ireland is a
turbulent and bloody one. The emerald green turf has all too
often been fed with the blood of victor and vanquished alike, so
that the possibility that the sites of ancient battles and affrays
may yield paranormal manifestations is hardly surprising.
Sometimes the events produce multi-phenomena; sometimes it
is the lone figure of some spectral warrior that alarms the
beholder.

In early times Ireland consisted of tribal kingdoms, where the
defence of one's lands and the honour of one's family were the
main reasons for strife. By the twelfth century Henry II of
England had assumed the lordship of Ireland, and the way lay
open for the Anglo-Norman conquest. However, the jurisdiction thus set up was less effective than had been anticipated. By
the time of Elizabeth I while, nominally, the royal authority of
the Tudors extended from Dublin throughout the whole
country, effectively the writ only ran within a relatively small
area about the capital, known as 'the Pale' – the term implying
an enclosure or limited area. Beyond this law-abiding and
tax-gathering area lay a hand divided into fifty or sixty regions,
each ruled by a chief or king, or by an Anglo-Norman lord. The
latter eventually adopted Irish names and intermarried with
Irish princely houses, thus becoming, some said, 'more Irish
than the Irish'. It was small wonder, then, that the land of
Ireland was a boiling pot of strife and dissension from time to
time.

Later came the insurrection of 1641 which soon merged into
'the war of three kingdoms', as Charles I fought to retain his
throne and 'divine right' against the English Parliament. In
Ireland during this troubled time hundreds of English settlers
were massacred, their lands stripped and their women and

children driven from home. It had become, in a sense, 'a holy war' as the fury of the Catholic Irish was unleashed upon the northern Protestant population. Ten years after these excesses Oliver Cromwell, the Lord Protector during England's interregnum, was to cite the murder of these unfortunates as the excuse for his barbarous deeds in Ireland. At the end of this terrible decade, one-third of the population lay dead, many had fled and the land lay wasted and unprofitable.

After Cromwell came the Williamite wars. James II was supported by Ireland against the Dutch Protestant prince, William of Orange, who now laid claim to the English throne by invitation from those in England who feared the resurgence of Catholic rule in England. Ireland once again became a battlefield as James Stuart and William of Orange pursued their claims. Among the notable events of this warring period were the Siege of Londonderry, the Battle of Enniskillen (1689) and the Battle of the Boyne (1690) which established for all time the supremacy of William of Orange as William III of England. He ruled the kingdom jointly with his wife Mary, to whom the crown would have legitimately descended in the normal course of events.

After a period of calm and genuine reform under the Irish parliament of Henry Gratton, which included legislative independence, once more disaffection flared and the Society of United Irishmen was born under its leader, Wolfe Tone, in 1791. A French attempt to support the rebels was launched, culminating in the landing of French troops in Bantry Bay in 1796. The rebellion in Ulster followed and the Rising of 1798, organized by Lord Edward Fitzgerald. Again these attempts came to nothing. By 1800 the Act of Union was in place by which Irelnd lost its own Parliament and instead sent a hundred members to Westminster and twenty-eight peers into the Upper House.

A century later, Ireland was to find itself, along with other European nations, having to contemplate the consequences of World War I. Thousands of young Irishmen from both north and south answered the call to arms and laid down their lives in the mud of Flanders' fields. At home in Ireland in 1916 came the Easter Rising, as those who sought Ireland's independence seized on England's preoccupations abroad and sought to make it 'Ireland's opportunity'. By the 1920s Ireland was in the grip of a bitter and destructive Civil War which turned brother against brother, until the eventual emergence of the Irish Free State under Eamon De Valera in 1930. What few foresaw at that time was that within a decade Europe would find itself embroiled in a world struggle against Fascism in World War II.

More than anything else, the troubled and bloody times over the centuries have imposed themselves on the spirit and psyche of the land and people of Ireland. The strange and often frightening reports by reputable witnesses mirror the physical and mental torment of those caught up in those 'old unhappy far off things and battles long ago' that bedevil the history and development of this island. They point with some poignancy to areas where the bones of the slaughtered still lie and to land still scarred by conflict.

The annals of Ireland are full of reports of terrifying deeds such as the following occurrence that took place, according to a contemporary account by a Mathew Paries, in Limerick in 1236:

> There appeared coming out of the earth, companies of armed men on horseback in battle array and encountered together. Sometimes they seemed to join in battle and fight violently; Sometimes they seemed to joust and break staves, as if it had been a tournament; the people of the country saw them at a distance, for the skirmish itself showed so lively that now and then they might see them come with their empty horses, sore wounded and bleeding, and likewise men mangled and bruised; and what seemed strange was that, after they had vanished, the prints of their feet appeared in the ground, and the grass was trodden in those places where they had been.

Maurice Lenihan, a nineteenth-century historian commenting on the same incident, said: 'The people were greatly troubled with a singular apprehension.' Possibly this was caused by the increasing wealth, privilege and power of the English settlers in Limerick. He attempts no explanation of the phenomenon apart from remarking that 'extraordinary fears occupied the people's imaginations, and the visions we must attribute more to their comparative ignorance than to reality'.

This is an interesting observation in the sense that it roots 'the fighting men vision' in the belief that one is dealing with psychological disturbances of the beholders and 'ignorance' of the peasantry, according to Lenihan. Yet similar events have occurred in other countries, as in the previously mentioned Battle of Edgehill. At Edgehill the witnesses were not 'ignorant peasants' but members of the Royal household sent to obtain evidence for no less a person than Charles II himself. One wonders if nineteenth century historians regarded Edgehill in a different light.

Built about the same time as the account of the 'fighting men of Limerick' was Castle Garde, Pallas Green, County Limerick. It was an ancient stronghold of the O'Gradys, a five-storey tower now linked to a more modern dwelling and claiming to be Limerick's oldest inhabited house.

This twelfth-century stronghold is haunted by a ghost that glides up and down the stone staircase and is identified by the sound of the rustle of a silken gown. This has earned her the name of 'The Lady in Silk'. The apparition was witnessed by the owners of the castle, a Mr and Mrs Hugh Thompson, in the 1950s. Mrs Thompson was disturbed by the swishing of silk in the early hours of the morning as she lay in bed in her third-floor room. She heard no footsteps, only the silken rustle on the stairs.

Local history speaks of a 'murder hole' in the tower, identified as a door on the third floor. Much like any other door, the difference is that this one leads to a space between the outer wall and inner door, so that whoever stepped through it fell fifty feet to his death at the foot of the hole.

Another chamber at the very top of the tower also has eerie associations, and few visitors would care to sleep in it. This, too, was believed to be haunted by 'The Lady in Silk'. With a dwelling of such antiquity it would be strange indeed if some paranormal happening had not attached itself to the castle. In fact there seems to be only one dark deed recorded. In the days of Elizabeth I, one of the owners of the castle was murdered by an Elizabethan officer who forcibly removed an old man's head from his body. It is difficult to make a connection, however, between this hideous deed and the soft and ladylike rustle of a silken gown.

To revert to the scene of battle, few have excited such comment and been kept so green in memory as the famous Battle of the Boyne, County Louth. The battle was fought in the summer of

1690 between the forces of William of Orange and James II of England. It is not at all surprising that over the centuries reports of phenomena have come from the area in and around the battle site on the River Boyne.

There have been reports of the sounds of marching men, of galloping horses and the rumble of carts in a secluded part of the woodlands where the Williamite army made camp during those momentous days. Beside the Boyne Water itself, at a point where William's artillery forded the river, there were reports too of shouts and screams and the general din of battle.

From Slane in County Meath, where a bridge crosses the river, there have been seen groups of phantom horsemen and the sight of men contending with each other. Other isolated incidents tell of lone horsemen seen on the road to the bridge, and one witness, a young girl in the nineteenth century, saw a large black cavalry horse in the wood near to the spot where William's army was said to have encamped.

A more gruesome manifestation was seen by a witness who perceived in the waters of the Boyne, not far from the ruined hermitage of Saint Erc, 'a number of bodies floating in the river'. The vision simply faded away after awhile, much to the witness's relief, for she saw too that the water was 'coloured red'. What a sad irony that one of the most beautiful stretches of water in Ireland should be scarred with the memory of this terrible slaughter, when the River Boyne ran crimson in the July days of 1690.

From such a great conflagration come stories of personal tragedy. One such story concerns the bansidhe seen at the Battle of the Boyne, in which the ancestors of the writer Elliott O Donnell fought. In fact according to tradition it was not one bansidhe but several bansidhes that keened at this battle. In McAnally's *Book of Wonders* we are told: 'Bansidhes were heard in the air over the Irish camp. The truth of the prophecy being verified by the death roll next morning....'

In the case of Elliott O Donnell's ancestor, he both heard and saw a bansidhe on the eve of battle. He was sitting at a camp fire with one or two brother officers and, as the night air was chill, he turned to lift his cloak which he had laid on the ground beside him. To his annoyance, it was no longer there. When he began searching for it, he saw a woman in a cloak, standing a little way off; she was dressed in costly garments and had a wealth of beautiful golden hair. Needless to say, it was unusual for a lady of rank to be found in such a location on the eve of battle. O Donnell noticed that she was trembling and clenching and unclenching her fists while she wept most bitterly. As he was about to approach her and speak with her, a brother officer called to him from the fire and asked why he had withdrawn from the group. As he watched, the woman slowly began to grow indistinct. Her eyes seemed to be fixed on a young boy, lying asleep and wrapped in his soldier's cloak. It seemed to O Donnell that the apparition bent over him and smoothed the boy's cheek, then laid her hand on his head. She moved to another sleeping soldier and then vanished. An hour later she returned, and this time O Donnell noted that others had noticed her and were uneasy, although nothing was said. As she vanished the second time, there came out of the air a sound of such piercing grief that the listeners froze in their tracks. O Donnell himself said that he was 'stunned by such indescribable grief'.

At the close of the Battle of the Boyne on the following day, many of O Donnell's friends and comrades lay dead on the banks of the river, among them the young, curly-haired lad to whom the bansidhe had come the evening before.

Apart from the earlier report of the 'fighting men of Limerick', there is a letter by one John Holme, dated 13 June 1640, which now forms part of the Smith Collection in the Royal Irish Academy. John Holme writes:

> For newes wee have the strangest that ever was heard of, there being inchantments in the lord of Castleconnells castle, four miles from Lymerick, several sorts of noyes, sometimes of drums and trumpets, sometimes of other curious musique with heavenly voyces, then fearful screeches and such outcryes that the neighbours cannot sleep. Priests have adventured there to bee, but have been cruelly beaten for their paynes and carried awaye they knew not howe, some ten miles and some four miles. Moreover, there were seen in lyke manner, after they appear to the views of the neighbours, infinite numbers of armed men both on foot and on horsebacke ...

It would seem that being a neighbour to Lord Castleconnell
had distinct disadvantages! 'Most of the inhabitants,' says
Holme, 'had seen an abundance of armed men, marching up
and down, but when they come up to them, they do not appear.'
Holme was much amazed at these events – 'these things are very
strange'. – and declares that he would go to Castleconnell to 'see
for himself'. His letter was sent to the Archbishop of Armagh,
who was then on a visit to Oxford, by a friend who was at pains
to point out in a covering letter that most of the information
gathered came from 'Cleargie and gentry' and that 'John Holme
was gentleman to the Lord Bishop of Limerick'. In other words,
the information did not come from the ignorant and
superstitious peasantry.

Limerick does seem to be predisposed towards multi-
phenomena, largely consisting of armed men. Perhaps it was the
troubled times that gave rise to such signs and wonders. It is
common tradition, expressed even by William Shakespeare, that
signs and portents may be expected in times of danger. The
Cromwellian pacification of Ireland was still to come at this
time, as was the siege of Limerick in 1651. Could it be that
'future events cast their shadows before'?

Killeadon House in County Mayo, one of the largest and most
beautiful of counties in the province of Connaught, was earlier
in this century to manifest some very strange phenomena to
members of the family. At the time some small modifications
were being made to the house, including the taking up of
flagstones in the front hall, and in particular the re-laying of one
large flag. Almost as soon as the work commenced the house
underwent a subtle change of atmosphere. The occupants began
to hear heavy footsteps, as though steel-shod feet walked the
hall, and there could be heard the rattle and jingle of horses' bits
or the scrape of weapons on stone. Even the animals whined and
grew fretful, as these disturbances sometimes went on for long
periods.

The two women occupants of the house were the aunts of
Captain Dermot McManus, the writer, and both were of stable
and sensible dispositions. However, the disturbances made
them uneasy. Accordingly, they sought help from the Church,
and an exorcist was duly brought to the house. One has to
wonder if this was a wise move, because after the prayers and

exhortations were over the feet ceased simply to tramp up and down and now made decisive moves towards the staircase and the room where the McManus ladies had retired for the night. One of the ladies, realizing that the feet were approaching the door, saw to her horror the handle slowly begin to turn. Despite the fact that the door had been locked, it now began to open very slowly.

Miss Emma McManus summoned up all her courage and cried in a loud voice, 'I forbid you to enter!' She did this three times, and on each occasion the door stopped moving. It seemed to her terrified sister that some battle of wills was taking place. Finally Emma exhorted their unwelcome 'visitor' again in a loud voice, 'I command you, in the name of the Blessed Trinity and by the Divine power of God, to go!' She repeated this three times, adding, 'Rest in the peace that only God can give you.' For a long time nothing happened, then somewhere in the house a door slammed and footsteps were heard retreating down a corridor. When they reached the end of the corridor they ceased and were never heard again.

When at last the workmen had lifted all the flags in the hall, they came across a small heap of human remains. Upon examination, these proved to be the bones of a young woman and a baby. Despite extensive enquiry, no one could explain the riddle of the bones or discover anything about the unknown mother and child. The remains were reverently re-interred in consecrated ground, and the disturbances ceased for good.

Another unusual event occurred in the same area of County Mayo as Killeadon House, the small village of Kiltimagh. This was a manifestation of the 'fear gortagh' or 'hungry grass', and it seemed to affect a stretch of road just outside Killeadon House. A well-documented account tells of the unfortunate experience of a Mr Michael Murphy, a man much known for good works and a member of the Town Council.

He had been attending a committee meeting at Killeadon one summer's evening, and when the meeting ended, Mr Murphy mounted his bicycle to go home. He had scarcely travelled fifty or sixty yards when he was overcome with a violent hunger, then his entire stomach seemed given over to cramps and searing pains. The unfortunate Murphy, gasping and reeling in agony, tottered down the road, leaning heavily for support on his trusty bicycle. His only thought was to get himself to a friendly door where he would find help. It was nearly three miles to his own home in Kiltimagh, and as he staggered along the road that journey must have seemed endless.

Finally he fell in at his own door and promptly collapsed, to his family's utter consternation. A visitor who was sharing the Murphy's simple supper, and who was wiser than the rest of the family as to the cause of the collapse, grasped the situation swiftly and with no more ado handed Michael Murphy a large, hot buttered loaf. Murphy fell on this and swallowed it in large gobbets, until not one crumb was left. He was helped to a seat, and without uttering a word he devoured a large plateful of ham, eggs and potatoes and drank a glass of buttermilk. Having mopped up all the food in sight, he promptly fell into a profound sleep from which he only wakened briefly as he was helped to bed. The next morning, Michael Murphy awoke none the worse for his bizarre experience.

Tradition has it that sometimes the unwary can step on a patch of the 'fear gortagh' or 'hungry grass', which is said to be a spot where some poor, starving creature in Famine times lay down to die of starvation. The victim experiences terrible hunger pangs that can only be assuaged by devouring what appears to be an incredible amount of food at one sitting.

Outside Castlebar in County Mayo is a hill with a cairn of stones that is known locally as the Bugler's Grave. It is believed to be haunted by the apparition of a young French soldier killed there in 1798.

The French expeditionary force under General Humbert arrived in Killala Bay in August, 1798 to render assistance to the men of the '98 Rising. Having captured Killala and Ballina, they advanced on Castlebar as evening was closing in and pitched their tents. The English forces, having been warned of the French advance, managed to get behind their advance troops. A young bugler, seeing the English soldiers, gave a warning on his bugle and in doing so was shot dead. The French beat off the attack on the hill of Turlough and captured the English raiding party.

The next day they advanced on Castlebar, where eventually the encounter known as 'the Races of Castlebar' took place and the English forces under General Lake were defeated. Eventually, however, the French General Humbert surrendered at Ballinamuck, and by the 23rd of September the rising in Connaught was over.

As for the young bugler, his comrades buried him on the hill under a large stone. Sometimes on summer nights the sound of a bugle is heard from the hill and the slight figure of the boy bugler may be seen. An alternative name sometimes used for his last resting place is 'Frenchman's Grave'.

Finally from County Mayo comes the tale of a bridge with a difference. While it may not be haunted in the usual sense, it does have a history of a curse lying over it. There are several versions of the story of the bridge at Bellacorick, and here are two that deal with the history of the bridge and the tradition linked to it.

Situated about ten miles from Crossmolina, the bridge is built of limestone and spans the Abhann Mor in the village itself. The building of the bridge commenced in the seventeenth century and was still underway at the beginning of the next century. It was truthfully foretold that the bridge would never be finished. It is said that musical tones can be produced if fingers are run along the stones of the northern parapet, and if you have any musical talent, you can play a tune or two on 'the musical bridge'. Sadly, the southern parapet produces no such tones.

The curse states that anyone foolish enough to complete the bridge will come to a bad end. Some years ago an unfortunate employee of the Mayo County Council had the task of fitting the last coping stone to the north end of the bridge. Within days he succumbed to an asthmatic attack. In 1920 another attempt to finish the bridge was made, but overnight the stone disappeared and was never found.

The local version of the story of Bellacorick Bridge runs like this: The actual building of the bridge took place in the 1820s. The builders were two brothers who were given a set time to finish the contract. Unfortunately, for all their good intentions they spent more time in the shebeen beside the bridge than actually working on its construction. The penalty for breaking the contract was transportation. When it became patently obvious that the work would not be finished in time, the frightened brothers disappeared overnight, leaving their widowed mother to shift for herself.

Locals say that she uttered the fateful 'Widow's Curse' and cursed both the bridge and the shebeen (a drinking den) for depriving her of her source of income. The curse appeared to be highly effective. The shebeen keeper and his family fell on hard times, and eventually the man of the house took to drink. As for the bridge, anyone attempting to complete the work that the widow's sons had left met with death or disaster. The bridge still lacks a final coping stone and, understandably, no one is too anxious to take it upon themselves to rectify the omission.

6   The Gormanstown Foxes

County Meath in the Province of Leinster was once part of the ancient province of Royal Meath, noted for its fertile pasturelands and rich in antiquities. In the county one finds the prehistoric site of Newgrange, with its passage tomb, the ecclesiastical remains at Ceannus Mor, from whence came the Book of Kells, and of course the royal seat of the High Kings–Tara. The River Boyne flows through the county and in the southwest forms the border with County Kildare.

The strange case of the Gormanstown foxes has something of the 'bansidhe' about it but, as far as one can ascertain, it is unique in the actual manifestation of a death warning. The present Gormanstown Castle was built in 1786 and a chapel was added the following year. It was a gracious place with a famed yew tree walk. The original castle was inhabited from early times by the Preston family, who had come from Lancashire in 1361. Sir Robert Preston fell in love with Gormanstown and established his home there, which, over the years, successive owners changed and improved. Eventually it was Sir Robert's great-grandson who became the first Viscount Gormanstown. The story of the foxes, however, does not occur until the time of the thirteenth Viscount. At least the story is not public knowledge before that time. The wife of the thirteenth Viscount, Lucrezia, had heard that before the death of the lord of Gormanstown the foxes on the estate kept vigil. However, being a level-headed lady, she dismissed this with a smile.

In the course of time, her husband fell gravely ill and came home to the castle to die. A few days before his death, Lord Gormanstown asked to be brought down into the library to sit in a chair and see for the last time the broad sweep of the acres of land he called home. While Lady Lucrezia was keeping him company on that fateful afternoon, she noticed a number of foxes sitting on the grass on the far side of the broad gravel drive around the castle. They did not appear to mind the close proximity of people, and when chased by the servants they would return after awhile and resume their watch in front of the library windows. It should be emphasized that these were not apparitional animals but solid, three-dimensional ones of blood and bone.

That night Lord Gormanstown suffered a relapse and died. Some days later, as the cortege left the castle for the burying grounds, Lord Gormanstown's daughter, the Honourable Mrs John Farrel, saw to her astonishment a number of foxes following the cortege through the fields alongside the road.

The fourteenth Viscount, Jenico, had been in his youth one of the witnesses to the foxes at his father's death. In 1907, when he was in his seventieth year, Jenico himself died in Dublin and his body was brought back to Gormanstown for burial. On this occasion the body was taken to rest in the chapel overnight, and his son, Colonel the Honourable Richard Preston, D.S.O., undertook to keep vigil with his father's coffin overnight in the chapel. His account of what happened is re-told in the Franciscan College Annual 1964. It makes curious reading:

> Some time around midnight or in the very early hours of the morning I became aware of a snuffling and whining at the door of the chapel at the west end – that is, the door opposite the altar. My brother at that time was breeding Irish wolfhounds and had a litter of puppies. Thinking that the yard gate had been left open and that the puppies had got out, I went and opened the chapel door ...

What Colonel Preston saw was to be imprinted on his mind for all time. In the light of the candles burning about the coffin he saw a group of foxes, some four or five in number, simply sitting and gazing into the chapel. They showed no fear at all of the colonel who, deeply upset, then turned and tried another door into the chapel. There too he found a 'guard' of foxes which he attempted to disperse with his foot. This proved unsuccessful – they simply moved a little ways off and sat or lay down again. This 'vigil' lasted until daybreak when, with one accord, the foxes disappeared. Colonel Preston, a brave and intelligent man, could find no rational explanation for the encounter. It came as little surprise to the Gormanstown tenantry, as it is on record on another occasion that an elderly man had remarked to a visitor up for a day's hunting in the district that 'he would get no sport, for the foxes were all away at the old lord's dying ...' Heads were shaken in rueful agreement.

To find a viable explanation would be difficult, even if one so presumed. However, two items of information do have a bearing on the story and add 'some flesh to the bones'. It had long been said that the reason for the foxes' vigil stemmed from an incident with an earlier Preston, in which the man concerned had shown great compassion to a pregnant vixen caught up in a hunt. The vixen's family had then demonstrated their gratitude in this curious fashion at their benefactor's death. Secondly, the Gormanstown armorial bearings show two foxes, one as supporter of the shield and the other as supporter to the crest. Thus, there must have been an ancient and significant connection between the family and the foxes. The castle is now Gormanstown College and under the jurisdiction of the Order of Saint Francis, a fact that, upon reflection, seems curiously appropriate.

County Offaly in Leinster Province is situated in the large central plain of Ireland. Unlike other counties known for their high and hilly regions, Offaly is a flat county and can lay claim to a substantial part of the great bog of Allen. The Grand Canal, too, flows through its central part. Offaly also contains the once great ecclesiastical centre of Christianity in Ireland, Clonmacnoise, and for those interested in ecclesiastical remains this is an area well worth visiting.

Two castles in Offaly warrant attention. One is Leap Castle, burnt down in 1923, which was the stronghold of the O'Carrolls, Princes of Ely, who had built the castle in the fourteenth century on the site of an earlier fortification. It is a castle mentioned in the Annals of the Four Masters in connection with an account of an abortive attempt by the Earl of Kildare to take the castle in 1515. Three years later he succeeded, half demolishing the castle in the process. His ownership ended in 1557, after which the O'Carrolls again laid claim to the castle until it was acquired by the Earl of Sussex.

The sixteenth century saw much bitter clan strife, with brother slaying brother within the precincts of the castle. Then the Crown took yet another opportunity to seize O'Carroll lands, and the castle became plantation property. Eventually it passed into the hands of the Derby family, when the young English Captain Derby fell in love with the O'Carroll heiress and the O'Carrolls took the young man hostage. The young pair planned to escape from their captors, but in the course of this escapade Derby killed the lady's brother. In the fullness of time Leap Castle passed into the lady's possession and, by marriage rights, became part of the Derby inheritance.

It seemed that the links between O'Carroll and Derby were doomed to be fraught with violence. In 1659 Jonathan Derby declared for the King and in the collecting for a war chest hid a great deal of treasure in the castle, with the help of two servants. When the deed was done, Derby took the precaution of murdering the two servants and burying their bodies in the grounds. By 1685 Derby himself was dead and the treasure lost, although his descendants continued in possession of Leap.

Even in those early days Leap Castle had a sinister reputation, and as the centuries rolled by and the catalogue of gruesome events expanded it came to be known as 'the most haunted castle' in Ireland. There was talk of a hideous 'thing', half-man, half-sheep, that stank to high heaven. And in the 1920s three cartloads of human remains were said to have been removed from the castle. In the dark and cavernous dungeons one could find all manner of ancient weaponry, as well as whole skeletons with rags still clinging to them. In the 'Bloody Chapel' above the Great Hall, a brother had once slaughtered a brother, and here an entry to a secret 'oubliette' was found – a sinister but very effective way of disposing of one's enemies.

Among the more individual apparitions of Leap was one that took the form of a tall woman, clad in scarlet who manifested at the dead of night. She appeared to possess some internal form of illumination which caused her to glow red at intervals. This apparition was never fully identified but was believed to be a member of the princely O'Carroll house, murdered in her bedchamber.

In later times, Lord Ross of Birr Castle, a close friend of the then Lord Derby, claimed he had personal proof that there were bodies bricked into the walls of Leap. Derby became so incensed at what he regarded as a scurrilous falsehood that he ordered one particularly 'suspect wall' to be opened up to disprove the theory. Unfortunately, when the wall was opened, three bodies found were bricked in upright positions, so he promptly re-bricked the wall again! In any event, Leap Castle had a powerful reputation for evil. Its annals speak of murders and tragic 'accidents', financial loss and personal grief. Within its halls, an atmosphere of horror and death is all pervasive.

There are a number of theories as to why some dwellings and the land about them seem to exert a malign influence on those who come in contact with them. One suggestion has to do with the actual material used in the building of any particular place – in the case of Leap, large quantities of stone. Stone can be regarded as having a living quality, capable of recording strong impulses and impressions. Stone may act like a recording tape, and when it gives out impressions and comes into contact with 'sensitive beings', events from the past can come to life once more and be felt by those whose ESP is particularly developed. Hence, there are places where some people may feel unaccountably depressed or fearful, or may have a full-blown paranormal experience. Leap Castle may have been such a place. It has also been suggested that Leap Castle lies directly above a powerful 'ley line', a veritable channel of power that draws its energy from the heart of Nature itself.

Clonony Castle is far less sinister, although every bit as interesting; a four square tower in a capacious bawn was used as a residence well into the nineteenth century. The castle has spanned at least four centuries, and when excavation work was done in the nineteenth century a number of artefacts were found, including some Elizabethan coins, a piece of body armour and some weaponry. It also revealed something infinitely more curious.

The men digging at the site discovered, some one hundred yards from the base of the tower, a limestone cave at the foot of a tree. When they dug in some ten to twelve feet they came to a mound of stones, beneath which a flagstone was concealed. When it was prised from its place they found a vault, and in it a coffin containing a quantity of bones, subsequently identified as female. There were possibly two bodies. The inscription on the coffin declared that these were the bodies of Elizabeth and Mary Boleyn, cousins to Anne Boleyn, Henry the Eighth's tragic Queen and mother of Elizabeth 1.

Why these two ladies should have been buried here poses a mystery. Certainly the Boleyn family had Irish connections, through marriage with the Carey family. A William Carey had married Mary Boleyn, Anne's eldest sister. There were also branches of the family in Inishowen and Dungiven, County Donegal. The earliest known Carey, Sir John Carey, had been an advisor to Richard II, but, falling from favour, he had been banished to Waterford and died there in 1471. Another branch of the Careys lived in County Antrim and gained notoriety in the nineteenth century through John Carey of Toomebridge, who is alleged to have attempted to murder a fellow Presbyterian minister. His tomb acknowledges his connection to the Boleyns and through them to the royal house of Tudor.

Yet the connection to Clonony is baffling. As for the apparition in the castle, it resembles neither the tragic Queen or her cousins. Instead, it takes the form of a man clad in very old fashioned garments who stations himself at the top of the tower. A witness in recent times described him as 'tall and thin, surrounded by a luminous haze'.

Near to Tara, once the religious and cultural hub of Ireland, with its ritual connections to the High Kings and its centre of Druidic worship, stands the castle of Skyrne.

The castle was built by a Norman knight, Adam De Feipo, towards the end of the twelfth century. It passed through much troubled times, and the fabric of the building suffered and fell into disrepair, but it was restored in the nineteenth century when the house was incorporated into the Old Keep. Nearby stands the ancient and mystical site of Cnoc Guile – 'the hill of the weeping' – and the vibrations and emanations from this spot add a number of strange incidents to the sum of 'mysterious Ireland'. Not the least of these events was the tragic tale of Lilith Palmerston.

By the 1740s the castle had become the residence of Sir Bromley Casway, who had as a ward a girl called Lilith Palmerston. After Lilith's parents were killed in an accident she had come to live with her guardian at Skyrne. Previously she had lived in Dublin. Lilith was a beautiful girl, and it was inevitable that she would excite much admiration among the wealthy men with whom she was acquainted. In particular she caught the eye of Phelim Sellers, a rich squire who made no secret of his admiration.

While she had been well treated in Dublin and enjoyed city life and its many social inducements, Lilith also spent a lot of time at Skyrne and had a close and loving relationship with her elderly guardian. Sir Bromley, who was frail in health, liked to have Lilith near him. Consequently it meant that the young girl lacked companionship of her own age and often was quite lonely at Skyrne. The attentions of Phelim Sellers made her both uneasy and irritated, and after suffering his importuning, Lilith decided to return to Dublin to remove herself from the pressures put on her at Skyrne. She feared and disliked Sellers. Rumour had it that Sellers, a widower, had so badly brutalized his young wife that she had died as a result of his treatment.

Unfortunately, Sir Bromley appeared to get on well with Sellers, who was always at his charming best when dealing with the old man, and thus he did not perceive Lilith's obvious distress when Sellers visited Skyrne. Thus emboldened, one afternoon as Lilith walked in the grounds, Sellers attempted to assault her. Fortunately she escaped harm, but now, thoroughly frightened and reluctant to distress her guardian, Lilith persuaded him to allow her to visit friends in Dublin. Reluctantly, Sir Bromley agreed. Sellers meanwhile had heard gossip in the servants' hall of Lilith's plans and, mad with lust, Sellers broke into the castle late at night and surprised Lilith in her bedchamber. Despite her desperate struggles, Sellers succeeded in raping her. Then, in a fury at her violent rejection of him, he strangled her.

Mindful of the retribution that must follow such an action, Sellers fled to Dublin and then to Galway, where justice caught up with him. He was arrested, charged with her murder and condemned to hang, the sentence being carried out in Clew Jail. Thus, it is the pathetic ghost of Lilith Palmerston that over the years has been seen at Skyrne, running frantically through the grounds to escape her seducer. The apparition wears a soiled and torn gown, and her hands clutch frantically at her throat. Sometimes the apparition gives vent to the most piteous cries.

Lilith is not the only phantom of this ancient place. Other apparitions include a tall figure wrapped in a cloak and accompanied by a shadowy dog, and a silent gliding figure of a man who walks in the garden in the fading light of day. Visitors to the castle are known to quicken their step and cast uneasy glances about them in the gloom as they catch the sound of a faint cry and sense a chill in the night air that they had not noticed before.

Sligo in Connaught is one of the most popular of the Irish counties, not least for the constant stream of pilgrims that go to pay their respects at the graveside of W.B. Yeats under the shadow of Ben Bulben. The inscription on his tomb reads: 'Cast a cold eye on life, on death, Horsemen pass by...'

Sligo's hills are imposing, with the Ox Mountains attaining 1,800 feet at their highest point, the Darry Mountains, north of Sligo town, and another range on the Leitrim border in excess of a thousand feet. Its seaboard stretches from Killala Bay in the west to Donegal Bay towards the north. It was at Rathmoy, facing the sea, that in the eighteenth century Lady Elizabeth Tully made her home. Fortunately, Rathmoy House had escaped the unwelcome attentions of Cromwell's army, and the Lady Elizabeth decided to spare no expense in greatly modifying and refurbishing the house. There had been talk of also building a 'model village' at Rathmoy's feet, but so much money was spent on the house that this plan had to be abandoned.

It was two years before the house was ready for Lady Elizabeth to take up residence, and almost at once the household became troubled by a curious manifestation. One evening, as Lady Elizabeth went up the stairs to her room, she became conscious of a curious 'slithering' noise which gave the impression of some quite heavy object being shunted down the staircase. The lady felt 'something' go past her, causing her to press herself flat against the banisters. The alarmed woman noticed too that the air seemed damp and chill, and once again she experienced the sensation and noises of a number of people struggling to transport a box or casket down the stairs, the object nudging against her legs. At this point, the lady fainted.

Lady Elizabeth, however, was a person of considerable stamina and determination, and in the morning she called the household together and questioned them on what she had experienced. Most seemed as baffled as she was, except for one old man who had worked in the house for forty years and more. He spoke of a time when, as a young boy, a secret room had been found in the house. The room had contained chairs and a table, and the skeleton of a man had been found seated at the table while another skeleton lay on the floor. The old man explained that the then owner of the house had had all the items in the room burned, and the remains gathered together and placed in a container. Then the room was sealed up again. The man had no idea if the remains had been hallowed before being interred in the box. 'It was never mentioned over all the years I have worked here,' he told Lady Elizabeth.

If the lady had hoped that this was the end of the matter, she was destined to be disappointed. Five times in three years, either she or a member of her family were caught up in a similar happening on the stairs. It became known as 'the Funeral Procession', and on the subsequent fourth and fifth occasions, the witnesses were so terrified that they suffered violent tremblings of the limbs, and had a tendency to suffer small but decidedly unpleasant accidents.

One evening in early May, a visitor who was feeling chilly went upstairs to fetch a shawl. When she was half way up the stairs she felt a hand as cold as death touch her, then she was forced back against the wall and grabbed by the throat. All the while beside her the slithering, bumping noises went on. The unfortunate woman fainted and would have sustained a nasty fall had not Lady Elizabeth, coming in search of her guest, caught the woman as she reeled. A doctor was called, but the woman lay unconscious for several days before being able to tell of her shocking ordeal.

A year later, almost to the day, another chilling event occurred. Lady Elizabeth herself was going upstairs, and as she rounded onto the return landing, she heard a dreadful choking sound and was immediately enveloped in a foul smell accompanied by a sensation of chill and damp. Some unseen force pushed her against the side of the stair, and she knew with a dreadful certainty that she was being manoeuvered into a position to be flung down the stairs. Even in her terrified state Lady Elizabeth had the presence of mind to fall flat on the stairs and cling to the spindles of the banister with all her might. In so doing, she undoubtedly saved her own life.

The shock of this incident caused a nervous collapse, and for weeks she lay in a semi-comatose state. Her physician ordered her to quit the house as soon as she was able and go back to Dublin. Lady Elizabeth obeyed but with great sadness, for she loved Rathmoy and now all her dreams were shattered. It is believed that she never visited Rathmoy House again.

Many people over the years took up the tenancy of the house, but few stayed long. Some even admitted to 'the terror of the stairs' and that it held such horror that they dared not stay. The tale of the secret room excited some imaginations, but none found it. One explanation of the phenomenon was that the object being bundled down the stairs was the coffin of an informer. Others said that it was the body of a drunken sea captain who had been robbed and murdered in the house by a companion. No one knows for certain exactly what was the dark and hideous secret of Rathmoy.

A gentler tale comes from the lovely Lissadel House near Drumcliff in County Sligo, home to the Gore-Booth family. The name comes from 'Lis' (a bawn or fort). Countess Markiewicz (nee Gore-Booth), one of the leaders of the 1916 Rising, lived at Lissadel during her early years. The two Gore-Booth girls were the toast of society and described by Yeats as 'Two girls in silk kimonos / Both beautiful, one a gazelle....' The house was built by Sir Robert Gore-Booth in neo-classical style and is truly a great house. With its tall windows letting in the light, the flowing classical lines could readily be appreciated. The long gallery connected the entrance hall with the reception rooms, and everywhere light flooded from above. The house enjoyed a magnificent view across Sligo Bay.

The grounds were spacious yet secluded, running down to the shore. One afternoon in the late 1980s, two Northern Ireland visitors were parked a little way from the house on a leafy path, pausing while one of them re-loaded his camera prior to going up to get a shot of the house. They were parked in a leafy, wooded area, intersected by small paths, and it was peaceful and pleasant on that sunny afternoon. Suddenly, in a clearing to the left of the car, two young women emerged from the trees, laughing and talking together. One of them was quite tall and slim, the other a little shorter but slender. They wore almost identical long fawn skirts, high necked blouses and large brimmed hats in what looked like straw. The taller of the two was carrying a large canvas folder tied with strings and a small canvas stool; the other had a handful of wild flowers and grasses. Without taking any notice of the car or its occupants, the two girls passed quite close in front of it and headed in the direction of the house; the couple in the car watched them disappear out of sight round a bend in the path.

The woman in the car was quite disturbed. Somehow, the face of one of the girls was faintly familiar and she mentioned the fact to her husband. He too was puzzled, but for an entirely different reason: as an amateur painter he had a good eye for colour and tone, and it seemed to him that the light surrounding the two girls was of a different quality than normal daylight. 'It was faded, somehow,' he told a friend later. 'It was, well, like an old photograph. I can't explain, but yes, faded ...' Some months later, while leafing through a book on the Easter Rising, he was to recognize the face of the tall slim girl – it was Constance Gore-Booth, the girl he had seen in the woods at Lissadell and now long dead.

Yeats concluded his poem about the sisters:

> Dear shadows, now you know it all
> All the folly of the fight
> With a common wrong or right.
> The innocent and the beautiful
> Have no enemy but time.

Another instance of paranormal manifestation arising from the 'troubles' in the early part of this century also comes from County Sligo. It happened on a stretch of road between Sligo town and the seaside resort of Bundoran, a road much frequented by tourists to this lovely county. The event that happened on this stretch of road was, sadly, common enough: a confrontation between the Royal Irish Constabulary and the IRA. The police suffered heavy casualties in the encounter.

In the 1920s a traveller on this road was horrified to find himself involved in a ghostly re-enactment of the ambush. He told friends later of how he could hear shouting, then the sound of rifles being cocked. Yet, although he could hear very clearly, he could see nothing. A similar incident in County Clare was also confined to auditory phenomena of a peculiarly distressing kind, including the sobs and groans of dying men.

One wonders if these incidents were aetheric echoes of past events. Or were the travellers telepathically aware of what had happened in these places? One would need to find out if the witnesses concerned already had prior knowledge of events, even if, consciously, they were not aware that they knew. It is possible that if that were the case, they could have been predisposed to be 'sensitive' to it.

7   The Orloff Whip

Tipperary in Munster is Ireland's largest inland county. It has many splendid natural beauty spots, including the Glen of Aherlow, the Blackwater Valley and, at Cashel, the famous and imposing Rock. There are numerous ruined castles and much of architectural interest, and near to the Cork border are the well known Mitchelstown caves.

Tipperary can also lay claim to one of the more unusual tales of the paranormal in that the chief focus of interest in this tale is a jewelled riding whip, 'the Orloff whip'. The house associated with this object of interest was Shallardstown and was built by a man called Cadogan Parrott in the early nineteenth century. He married and had two daughters, Angelica and Rosaleen. Tragedy was not far away, however: Mrs Parrott took her own life, closely followed by the death of her husband, and the beautiful house at Ballymacorthy devolved upon the elder daughter, Angelica.

Angelica too was to have her share of sorrow. The man she fell in love with showed a preference for her younger sister, Rosaleen, who he married in 1837. Conscious that she was less than popular at home, Rosaleen persuaded her young husband, Dagan Ferriter, to take her travelling in Europe. Shortly after they left, Angelica herself went to London.

In London she was to meet a member of the Diplomatic Corps, a Russian prince called Nicholas Orloff. The couple fell in love and were married, spending their honeymoon in St Petersburg. On their return to the prince's next posting, in Paris, disaster struck when Nicholas succumbed to a short illness. The anguished widow, who had scarcely been a wife, returned to Ireland and Shallardstown. She dismissed all her old servants and contented herself with the services of her butler, a man called Creed. The house became for Angelica a prison where no one visited or even came to enquire after her for months on end.

Her sister Rosaleen had been deeply saddened by her sister's loss and returned to Ballymacorthy to see what consolation she might offer. But Angelica refused to see either her or her husband Dagan. They bore this patiently enough, and it was known, of course, that at Angelica's death Rosaleen would inherit the house at Shallardstown. After some time had passed it seemed that the Princess Orloff might be lightening the burden of her self-imposed reclusion. Every afternoon she took a drive in her carriage, with Creed acting as her coachman. The drive lasted for only an hour, during which the curious could see Princess Orloff seated in her carriage and holding in her hands a beautiful riding whip that had been a honeymoon present she had brought home with her from St Petersburg. This single daily drive went on for some years, and while the princess showed no signs of wishing to entertain or be reconciled with her sister, she never deviated from her routine. Meanwhile, Rosaleen and her husband, who had been dependent on Angelica for a small financial stipend, fell on hard times. Angry at the way in which his wife Rosaleen had been treated, Dagan Ferriter finally decided that he would go up to Shallardstown and confront Angelica. Swallowing his pride, he and two friends rode up to the 'Big House' and demanded to see its mistress.

They were received by the now elderly butler, Creed, who under pressure broke down and told them the most extraordinary tale. It seemed that his mistress had in fact died eleven years earlier. It was on her strict instructions that her corpse was placed in the carriage and driven about for all to see. The tragic and disturbed woman, who had never forgiven her sister for having the happiness of a married life that had been denied to her, had been determined to keep Rosaleen from her inheritance as long as she possibly could. As for the jewelled whip, she had told Creed to get a case made for it and to display it on a table in the entrance hall. Furthermore, she laid a curse on it that would prevent anyone else handling it.

Having seen to the discreet burial of Angelica, Rosaleen and her husband moved into Shallardstown. Within a year they were both dead, cause unknown. The whip, however, remained in the hall. The house was inherited by a distant cousin and then passed into the care of a religious order in 1896. Yet over the years, strange accounts of the Orloff whip began to circulate. An apparition was seen on a number of occasions, standing in the entrance hall, surveying the whip. Sometimes, about three o'clock of an afternoon, the sound of a carriage could be heard drawing away from the front door. Later, when the house stood vacant, the ghostly figure was still seen in the hall and on the stairs by those who looked after the house. One such caretaker declared that it was not uncommon to come into the hall about four o'clock in the afternoon to find the lid of the whip case open and the whip lying a little askew, as though someone had picked it up.

One of the most notable houses in County Tipperary in the eighteenth century was Longfield House, built by the Long family in 1770. The house eventually was acquired by Charles Bianconi, known as 'The King of the Irish Roads'. Bianconi had been born in Tregolo, Italy, on 24 September 1786, one of five children. Although he had a happy boyhood, the young Carlo always had his eyes fixed on high adventure beyond his own safe world. And so it was that in 1820 Carlo became apprenticed to a printmaker, Andrea Faroni, who also specialized in the mounting and selling of prints. Like many another Italian artisan, Faroni was determined to come to the British Isles to try his fortune. Carlo, now in his sixteenth year, went with him. They headed for Ireland, where Carlo soon demonstrated his ability as a salesman of religious prints and pictures. He was shrewd enough to realize that while he was a good salesman, he never would be a good craftsman.

As he grew older, Carlo's business skills increased and he became the owner of a shop in Clonmel, while his very lively mind made him consider all manner of other business ventures. He made friends easily, and among those friends was Daniel O'Connell, 'The Liberator'. This was a friendship that would last for a lifetime. As time went by, Carlo observed that while he had the money to indulge in a horse and trap for business and pleasure, many people less well off had to walk for there was no convenient form of public transport. Another problem was the irregularity of the postal system. The mail was carried in coaches that ran on the main trunk roads and the proprietors of such a coach service were more concerned with their profit than the convenience of their service to the public.

Charles Bianconi was to change all that. In July, 1815, the first Bianconi car took to the road between Cahir and Clonmel. For the very first time, His Majesty's Mails were carried by an Italian printer. The Bian Cars, as they were known, went from strength to strength. Soon they were covering 225 miles of road and extending in every direction. They were fast, clean and, more importantly, they ran on time. His workers were good and honest, with an affectionate respect for their employer; his horses, his pride and joy, were healthy and well cared for. By 1864 the passenger traffic alone was worth £27,731, and the mail contracts another £12,000. In addition, Bianconi had acquired a wife and family and a great estate of nearly 5,000 acres. His fellow citizens in Clonmel had honoured him by twice making him mayor, and he was also a J.P. He lived to a ripe and healthy old age and died in 1875. He had grown gradually frailer and more dependent on those around him in those last months, but his mind remained sharp and clear.

There is a strange and very moving story about the passing of Charles Bianconi, and it has been so well authenticated that even today people are hesitant about being alone on the main drive to Longfield House after dark. For they will say that when Bianconi lay dying, his beloved horses came to fetch him. He died at a quarter to five on the morning of 22 September 1875, two days before his eighty-ninth birthday. It was a fine autumnal morning, and to the weary watchers at his bedside it seemed fitting that he should pass with the sound of birdsong in his ears. Suddenly, to everyone's astonishment, there could be heard the sound of galloping hooves, emanating from the gravel sweep below the bedroom windows. The hands in the stableyard hurriedly checked the horses and the gates, but no horses were loose and the gates were locked. Yet the horses of Longfield could still be heard, as wave upon wave of galloping and trotting hoofbeats came by the windows. Charles Bianconi heard them too, for he opened his eyes and smiled as he appeared to listen to the familiar sound. Slowly the hooves got fainter and fainter until they were gone entirely, and Charles Bianconi went quietly to his rest.

Death warnings come in a variety of ways, apart from the bansidhe or 'black dog'. They can take the form of lights, foosteps or, the most common of all, raps and knockings. Many families are followed by knockings – sometimes on the door, sometimes in the house on walls and furniture. A Belfast woman told of raps on a particular table, which were always regarded as a warning. In Westmeath a family living in Emo House, a very fine old building, were troubled with knocking on the front door. At first the occupant assumed it was someone having a joke at his expense. Then, later in the evening, he found himself in the position of being able to see the outside of the front door just as the knocks commenced. While he could distinctly hear the sound, he did not see the knocker on the door move.

Another night, while expecting his brother to return home, he heard the knocks again, and this time the noise was so persistent that he actually went down and opened the door. There was no one there. The man had not seen fit to mention the knocking to anyone else, no doubt for fear of being thought foolish. But one day, in conversation with one of the outdoor workers, the worker confessed that he too had heard the knocking, although he slept at the far end of what was a large house. The noise persisted for some months then disappeared as mysteriously as it had come. It did not, fortunately, have any tragic sequel, much to everyone's relief. But local people believed it to be the restless wanderings of some earlier occupant of the house.

Another curious incident took place in the house one evening when the family were entertaining a clergyman as a guest, one who in fact was interested in the paranormal. As they sat in the drawing-room late that evening, the door into the hall slowly opened very wide, all by itself, and then just as slowly closed by itself. The three witnesses to this affirmed that there was no wind or any other reason that could cause a heavy double door to behave in this fashion. Needless to say, the party broke up quickly and a very sober threesome made their way to bed!

It is useful to recall, if one is investigating events that have a paranormal background, that anything that can be produced in the material world can be duplicated paranormally, no matter how bizarre this may be. During the Second World War, or 'The Emergency' as it was called in the south of Ireland, many of the larger houses were taken over for billeting troops and for storage. An officer in an army unit at this time related the following incident in one such house. A few days after taking up his new billet, as he was sitting quietly reading in the room used as the Orderly Officers quarters, from across the hall he heard the unmistakable sound of a game of billiards in progress. Overjoyed at having been sent to a billet with this very attractive amenity, the young officer went across the hall to make enquiries of the billiard players. To his astonishment, when he opened the door the room was not only in total darkness but empty of any furniture. The moment he shut the door the sound of the gentle clicking of billiard balls could be heard, along with the rattle of cues. Then, suddenly, there was a sharp noise, as if someone had flung down a cue onto the ground, and all the other noises ceased. To his infinite relief, upon enquiry he found that another officer as well had heard the 'game' being played. Again, one can but conjecture that the young men had picked up the aetheric echoes of a game that had, at some time, been played in the house. The sounds had been captured for all time, so that those who may have unconsciously exercised their ESP would hear it.

The county of Wexford has one particular claim to fame in that it was the first county in which the Normans landed in 1169. Thereafter Wexford had a dark and turbulent history, not the least during the '98 Rising when the towns of Wexford, Enniscorthy and New Ross distinguished themselves with the ferocity of their pikemen during the insurrection. It is a fertile and lovely county in the southeast of the country, and its coastline faces not only the Atlantic but St Georges Channel and the Irish Sea as well. There is a variety of information on paranormal activity in the county, and one of the best documented accounts of a poltergeist comes from Enniscorthy town.

Ireland has a distinguished history in relation to the poltergeist phenomenon, from quite early times. If one consults the files of the London Society for Psychical Research, one may be quite surprised at the intensity of investigation that has, over the years, taken place in Ireland. Poltergeists are a 'popular' manifestation, and are at times physically dangerous. They can, as their Germanic name implies, be truly 'noisy, boisterous spirits'. Although the exact nature of this phenomenon has given pause for thought, the theories range from 'little demons' on the perimeter of our world to spontaneous bursts of natural energy, channelled through a human being who is quite unaware of his or her part in the event. As a form of kinetic energy, would it then be capable of moving objects, producing water or performing other acts such as levitation? Perhaps. One has to preserve an open mind and judge each happening on its own merits. This is a fascinating area of research and one of the more mysterious manifestations to be found in 'mysterious Ireland'.

The Enniscorthy poltergeist operated from a private house in Court Street in the presence of a family called Redmond and a local journalist named Nicholas Murphy. Those most involved were a pair of young men who lodged in the house, John Randal and George Sinott. Number 18 Court Street had only been recently built in that summer of 1910.

The incidents began in customary fashion with knocks and bangs, footsteps heard on the stairs and furniture moved about in the bedrooms. The main disturbance took place in the room occupied by Randal and Sinott, who were on several occasions thrown out of bed along with their bedclothes. And for them to hear a 'drumming effect' issuing from the bedstead was not unusual. From time to time the bed itself, minus one castor, was lugged about the room by an unseen force.

Nicholas Murphy, a local journalist, heard the gossip about Number 18 and received permission to spend the night as an observer in the bedroom. He saw with his own eyes the men being thrown out of bed, mattress and all, while the housemaid Bridget said that she saw a chair performing a variation of a 'Slip Jig' in the middle of the floor, all by itself. Such was the fame of the Enniscorthy poltergeist that it was investigated by no less a personage than Sir William Barret of Dublin, a very well known surgeon and member of the Psychical Research Society. As a scientist of some repute he came to Wexford to investigate on behalf of the SPR in London. He listened carefully to all the witnesses and was very impressed by the frankness and honesty of the two young men. The family told of the footsteps on the stairs, the drumming sounds and the sight of inanimate bedclothes rising up and snaking through the bars of the brass bedstead by themselves while the terrified young lodgers cowered on the floor.

Understandably, Randal and Sinott gave in their notice and moved to a more peaceful lodging. It would seem that with their departure, or more particularly the departure of John Randal, the house settled down and everything returned to normal. Sir

William expressed the opinion that Randal was the 'radiant centre' that attracted these outbursts of energy. When, as requested, John Randal wrote a full account of all that had occurred at Court Street, he concluded by saying, 'I never believed in ghosts before that, and I think it would convince the bravest man in Ireland.' He was probably right!

The dwelling known as Loftus Hall lies on the east side of the River Suir and is believed to have been built on the site of a fortified mound associated with Strongbow. In the surges of fortune over the centuries between Irish chief and English settler, the house fell into the hands of the Loftus family after the 1660s and the family subsequently expanded and improved the site. By the eighteenth century the hall had become the family home of Charles Tottenham, an Irish M.P. This gentleman rejoiced in the nickname of 'Tottenham of the Boots', on account of a spectacular ride he had made to the Parliament in Dublin to give his casting vote to the Government, thus saving it £80,000 pounds. During the time that the House was in summer recess, it was Tottenham's custom to give house parties, no doubt to boost his political popularity as well as to curry favour with the great ones of state.

The fair sex were always well represented at these parties, and many a romance flourished at the hall. At one of these parties Tottenham's daughter fell in love with a member of the landed gentry who, unfortunately, did not find favour in her father's eye. His daughter was adamant about her love but Tottenham was stubborn. He flatly refused the young couple's request to wed, and his daughter went into a decline and subsequently died. It would be gilding the lily to say that she died of a broken heart, but it does seem to have been the popular explanation.

Some considerable time after the girl's death, her father was once again entertaining, this time giving a shooting party for his friends. One young sportsman, while cleaning his gun in the Loftus Hall gun-room, received an unexpected visitation. Just as he was finishing up, the door opened and in walked a young girl in a white gown. She ignored the startled visitor, walked up the gun-room and disappeared through the wall. The young man's description of her was recognized by the family, and subsequently she was seen on several occasions by the family. In the end, Tottenham asked the parish priest to perform an exorcism.

Why she had first appeared to this particular young man is open to question. Perhaps he had some connection to her lost love. Indeed, it may be that the young man was in a particular state of mind that caused his ESP to activate and so enabled him to 'see' the unhappy girl.

There is another story about Loftus Hall which concerns a party of card players who were indulging in a hand or two one stormy night when a stranger came to the door and asked for shelter. He seemed to be of 'the Quality', so the master of Loftus invited him to join in the game and he even partnered Loftus's daughter. A clap of thunder startled the party, and the daughter accidentally dropped her cards on the floor. As she bent down to retrieve them, she noticed to her horror that the guest had cloven hooves instead of feet. She screamed, the guest sprang up and all the candles went out. When order was restored the 'guest' was gone, but the daughter was in a grievous mental state.

Eventually she was confined to her room where she muttered or screamed and, refusing all comfort, huddled in a corner on the floor. Eventually she died, and it was said that she was so deformed by sitting in one position for years that a special coffin had to be made to contain her body.

The room she had occupied became known as the 'Tapestry Room', and it was said to be haunted. Few people passed the night in any comfort there, as the apparition of the girl would manifest in the most tragic way. After many years, when the house lay empty, an intrepid priest once more sought to exorcise the house. He succeeded, but not without a great deal of trouble. An inscription on a tombstone in the local churchyard reads: 'And Father Broaders, the best of all, Who banished the ghost of Loftus Hall.'

The surrounding area has a number of interesting features. In the eighteenth century the well known pair of writers and travellers in Ireland, Mr and Mrs S. C. Hall, tell in their three-volume work on Ireland of the Tower of Hook. It stood at the entrance to the narrow peninsula between Waterford harbour and Bannow Bay. By the Halls' time it had been converted into a lighthouse, but it was thought originally to have been erected by Rose McCrume, the founder of New Ross. The tower allowed fine views over the surrounding countryside. Its last warden, who lived to be a hundred, was said to have died at his post. For many years it was said that the old man still could be seen 'on watch' at his beloved tower home. The Halls were at pains to point out that at nearby Bag-na-Bun 'the first hostile Englishman trod Irish soil' and that 'at the extremity of the broad bay stands the abbey of Tintern'.

The name 'Tintern' conjures up not only the peace and tranquillity of this corner of Wexford but the gracious beauty of the mother house, in Monmouthshire in Wales. Sometimes the abbey is called 'Tintern de Voto' for it came about as the result of a vow made by William le Mareschall, the Earl of Pembroke, in the thirteenth century. It is said that, while travelling from Wales to Ireland, William was caught up in a great storm and feared both for his ship and his life. The earl beseeched God to spare his life, and he vowed that wherever the ship made land, there he would build a church as thanksgiving.

By God's providence they were set down at Bannow Bay, and there William built his abbey. When it was finished, he sent to Tintern Abbey in Wales to come and found a Cistercian community at Tintern de Voto. Later, secular buildings were added and a castle joined the abbey in the green vale of Wexford. One might well wonder what kind of paranormal phenomenon would disturb such a sanctified spot. Yet over the centuries there have been tales of torchlight processions, and the brothers, close cowled and singing their office, have been seen entering the great door of the abbey long after Tintern had become a partial ruin. As late as 1991 men working on the site heard the sound of singing coming from the abbey, and if one visits Tintern one does get the impression of being watched.

In company with many another religious house, Tintern's community was dissolved in 1533 and the lands granted, for services rendered, to Sir Anthony Colclough to hold 'in capite' on the order of Elizabeth I for an annual rent of 26 shillings and 4 pence. The Colcloughs became so well integrated with the local Irish that it was said that they were 'more Irish than the Irish', but they had one disadvantage. They were one of the few families in both England and Ireland who were said to be under 'the curse of fire and water' that devolved upon anyone in possession of original church lands. One local tale says that Sir

Anthony in fact murdered the friars at Tintern when he came to take up his ownership. Another tale says that the Colcloughs were cursed because they meddled in fairy matters by levelling a fairy rath or fort.

Sir Caesar Colclough fell foul of the little people, it is said. He was betrothed to the Redmond heiress of the Tower of Hook, and when he had to make a journey to England his loving fiancee said that she would burn a candle in her window to guide him home. On Colclough's return to Ireland his boat was steered towards the Tower of Hook. The fairies, alas, had sent the lady to sleep and put out the light, and the unfortunate Colclough ran his boat onto the rocks and perished, his body being found on the shore. It was his grieving fiancee who is said to have transformed the tower into a lighthouse to safeguard other mariners.

Wexford, for the most part, is remembered historically not for its grieving ghosts but for its part in the Wexford Rising of 1798, a savage and bloody affair by all accounts. The rebellion began on 27 May when Father John Murphy led his men against the North Cork Militia. The sheer raw courage of these men against professional troops rallied the countryside to their cause, and for a short time the rebels appeared to be winning. To join forces with their fellows in neighbouring counties, the Wexford men had to capture New Ross. The town therefore, was attacked on 5 June 1798, but the forces of the Crown stood firm against what has been described as a 'frenzied assault'. After twelve hours of fighting, the rebels were repulsed with a casualty count of over a thousand men.

This defeat was the turning point in the Rising, and when fresh troops were dispatched from England the rebels' strength, if not their resolve, faltered. By 21 June their main stronghold at Vinegar Hill was captured and the rebellion was over. In those final, dreadful days the insurgents held Wexford town for over a month. The 'reward' for the citizens of Wexford was typical of the savagery of the day. One hundred citizens were piked to death on the bridge of the town and their bodies hurled into the river.

County Wicklow in Leinster is quite mountainous, the Wicklow mountains extending from the Dublin border in the north to the Wicklow border in the south with the highest point being

Lugnaquilla at 3,000 feet. Perhaps the best known of Wicklow beauty spots is the vale of Glendalough (Glen of two lakes) with its important ecclesiastical remains, and for those who are lovers of the poetry of Tom Moore the beautiful Vale of Avoca with its Meeting of the Waters never fails to charm the visitor. Wicklow contains many fine houses, including the Powerscourt Demesne with its impressive waterfall. Those in search of either scenic interest or historical remains will find Wicklow very rewarding.

Today Poulaphouca is best known for the large reservoir it contains, but the name will give those interested in fairy lore much more to think about. 'Pol an Phuca' means 'the puca's Pool', the puca or pooka being a species of fairy horse – a creature given from time to time to terrorizing mortals. It also is known as a 'shape shifter', for it is believed that it can change into an ass, goat or dog. The poet Yeats thought it could even assume the shape of an eagle. Traditionally, it is black in colour with fiery eyes, and obviously it has some affinity with the 'black dog'. The English 'Puck', while able to shape shift, is much more endearing. It is a spirit of earth, quite unlike the 'puca' which has a reputation for bringing evil and death in his wake. In the northern counties of Ulster the 'puca' takes the form of a shaggy black pony with blazing eyes. It has the iniquitous habit of occasionally taking some unfortunate for a ride on its back, said to be enough 'to scare the wits from a wise man'.

Many Irish place names incorporate 'pooka' as an indication of the creature's presence there, and the names 'rath' or 'Lis' may be the pooka's haunts as well. The country children, when gathering wild fruit in late autumn, are careful to gather the blackberries before the pooka breathes on them, because they then become inedible.

A curious episode to do with the pooka came to light in 1952. A young lady called Margo Ryan was walking back to her home with a large can of butter-milk. It was a quiet summer evening and she was quite content to walk up the lane alone. Suddenly, she found to her surprise that she had the company of a large, handsome dog who loped happily beside her and seemed anxious to be friends. After awhile, Margo put out her hand to pat the dog, but no matter how she tried the dog always seemed to be out of reach. A short time later the dog moved away from her. It seemed to grow and to change shape into a larger animal. Then it vanished altogether.

Another pooka surfaced in County Roscommon, near Ballaghadreen, in the early part of the century. Again, it was a young girl who saw it, and, again, it first took the form of a large black dog. It stood as high as her shoulder but exhibited no hostility. The girl nevertheless was most uneasy to have this strange creature walking alongside her. Finally the dog reached an iron gate. To the girl's horror it seemed to grow larger and shift its shape; then it walked right through the closed gate and vanished. The girl ran screaming all the way home, but when she told the story her mother flatly refused to believe that she'd seen the pooka. Some time later a collector of folk lore was in the district and, upon hearing the girl's account, he showed her a picture of the pooka. 'That's it!' she told him. 'That's exactly what I saw!'

From the fairy creature in the form of the pooka, the discerning traveller (particularly if he is also a geologist) may find the wild but attractive Glenmalure of particular interest. It is here that two moraines (marginal lines of debris left by a glacier) formed during the glacial period. Although a remote and lovely spot, the glen has a troubled history and had a part to play in the savage events of the 1580s.

At that time the royal troops under Lord Grey de Wilton attempted to penetrate the valley and were slaughtered in great numbers by the men of Feagh McHugh O Byrne. Later, in the Rising of 1798, an Irish leader named Holt retreated into the upper part of the glen until, seeing that his resistance was hopeless, he surrendered to Lord Powerscourt at Enniskerry on 10 November 1798.

In the present century, campers in the glen have felt an eerie and hostile presence. Once or twice witnesses have reported a number of twinkling lights, such as might be expected from an army huddled about its camp fires. The atmosphere becomes hostile and brooding and feels so alien that sensitives who have stayed the night liken it to the feeling sometimes sensed in one of Scotland's most tragic glens, Glencoe.

Another memorable battle of the 1798 insurrection was that of Moretown, near New Ross, fought on 20 June 1798 between the insurgents under Father Philip Roche and the English troops commanded by the illustrious Sir John Moore. It was a confused and indecisive encounter that nevertheless brought heavy casualties to both sides. Finally the Wexford men retreated to re-group. The dead of both sides were buried in the fields where they fell, and the areas about the townlands of Stoneen and Raheenduff became war cemeteries.

The paranormal manifestation connected to the Moretown massacre concerned the apparition of a Hessian trooper who is said to appear under a tree near Moretown cross. The reason for this location is that, like the French bugler at Castlebar, his comrades buried the Hessian where he fell.

The most extraordinary phenomenon did not occur, however, until fifty years after the battle on 20 June 1848. On the anniversary of the battle, an elderly woman was driving her donkey and cart home in company with her small grandson. When she got to the Moretown bridge she saw with terror that the bridge was occupied by a ghastly horde of fighting men, armed with pikes and swords. In a dreadful silence they contended together, their dead faces lit by a frightful aura of light. Calling on all the saints in the calendar, the woman whipped up her terrified donkey and fled through their midst, urging her grandson to close his eyes and pray.

When the traumatized pair arrived home, they told their astounded relatives that they had seen the men of Moretown who had fought at the bridge fifty years before. The child never recovered from his ordeal and died a short time later, but his grandmother lived for some years and told her story to whoever wished to hear it. In 1990 on Vinegar Hill some visitors to the hill heard about them the rumbling of carts, the sounds of shouts and cries and a noise of many people gathered together. They saw nothing, except for one man who thought for a brief instant he saw what he took to be a pike flash down onto the ground. This manifestation was seen by others some six months later, and a similar description was given. The ghosts of Vinegar Hill, it seems, walk still.

The question it poses to paranormalists is whether the combination of violent death and its attendant anguish and despair can produce a particular 'aura' that is felt by those sensitive to such atmospheres. What we can personally vouch for is that fear and despair are among some of the most powerful emotions known to man, and those emotions may very well outlive the physical body.

Northern Ireland

8 Buttoncaps Well

A county of Northern Ireland, Antrim lies close to Scotland with the nearest point of proximity being Torr Head, only twelve miles from the Mull of Kintyre. One of the tourist attractions of Antrim is its Coast Road, which ranks among some of the finest in Europe. Connected to it are the lovely Nine Glens, possessing great scenic splendour, and in particular Glenariff with its spectacular waterfalls. Here too along the coast is the famous Giant's Causeway. Antrim also contains the capital of Northern Ireland, Belfast, standing on the River Lagan. It is a county rich in history and archaeology and, in paranormal terms, has a vast diversity of information extending up to the present day.

At Carrickfergus in County Antrim stands one of the most imposing of Norman castles in Ireland. The castle is built on a rock jutting out into the grey waters of Belfast Lough, and it is here that it is traditionally maintained that Fergus, founder of the royal house of Scotland, was drowned. This belief is reflected for all time in the town's name, Carrickfergus (Rock of Fergus). The castle itself was built at the beginning of the thirteenth century by the knight John De Courcy or by his kinsman, Hugh De Lacey. It has seen many famous and infamous visitors come and go. King John slept here, William the Bruce had brief possession of it, and it was beneath its walls that William of Orange landed on his way to the Battle of the Boyne. The castle has many notable features and is well worth a visit. One of its dungeons once held as prisoner the chief Con O Neill of Clandeboye, who escaped from it by means of ropes that his ever thoughtful wife had provided for him, concealed in a cheese. Then there is 'Buttoncap's Well', some thirty-seven feet deep, that is alleged to be haunted by the ghost of a soldier called Robert Rainey, a native of the district.

Rainey was a wild fellow, and he had for a friend a man called Tim Lavery, belonging to the same regiment as himself. Rainey also had a girl called Betsy Baird, from the nearby district of Whiteabbey, who was far enough smitten to promise Rainey that she would marry him. What Rainey did not know was that the wayward Betsy had another lover, a Colonel Jennings, who was brother to Rainey's own colonel. One night as Rainey was returning to the castle from Betsy's, he heard and saw enough to convince him of the 'two-timing' that was going on between Jennings and Betsy. The very next night he met his rival on the road to Whiteabbey and after a short altercation ran Colonel Jennings through with his sword.

It was a great mischance that Rainey and his friend Lavery were uncommonly alike, and the dying Jennings mistook Rainey for Lavery on the dark road. Even more unfortunate was the fact that Jennings lived long enough to mistakenly identify his murderer as Tim Lavery, not Robert Rainey. Meanwhile the real assassin had hurried to his quarters, cleaned his weapon and gone to bed. The wretched Lavery was arrested and tried and, despite his frantic protestations of innocence, was found guilty and hanged. The coward that had been his friend only revealed the truth of the matter some years later, when he was lying on his own deathbed.

Lavery is said to have cursed Robert Rainey as he mounted the scaffold, and in this curse he included his comrades who had not come to help him. He told them that they would have no peace for killing an innocent man: 'Not anyone will have rest; I will be revenged!'

And so it was that the apparition of Lavery haunted the castle yard, especially near the castle well. The name Buttoncap's Well came to be used, as this was the nickname given to Lavery by his comrades because he always wore a large button central to the cockade on his cap. Many people over the years have attested to seeing 'Buttoncap's Ghost', but no one has ever seen an apparition of the truly guilty party, Robert Rainey.

Not far from Carrickfergus is the busy port of Larne, from which the ferries to Scotland run daily. Larne also has strong connections to the linen trade, and indeed in neolithic times it was the heart of a flourishing flint trade. The town stands at the doorway to the Glens of Antrim and the beginning of the Antrim Coast Road.

Up until some years ago the town also held Invermore House, a nineteenth century dwelling that passed from private ownership to public development. During the latter years, the house was occupied by three ladies, two Misses Thompsons and a Miss McClane, together with a delightful variety of canine companions. The house had been built in the early 1800s, with additions about 1845. The original owners were the Casement family of County Antrim, one of whom was Roger Casement. The local graveyard contains family memorials, and also those of the Howden and Fisher families who had occupied the house.

In the summer of 1981 Miss Thompson telephoned the author, and asked if she would come and advise her on certain 'happenings' in the house. Even while speaking to the author on the telephone, Miss Thompson was startled by the sound of the front door opening and closing, only to find on investigation that the door was shut and locked and she was alone in the house. This was typical of the incidents that took place at Invermore, in which drawers and cupboards were ransacked, furniture moved about and footsteps both of animals and people heard in the house. The author can vouch for the door episode while on the telephone, as a door was heard distinctly to close, or be slammed shut.

From subsequent conversations it also transpired that at least two of the women had heard what they took to be the bansidhe. It is of passing interest that Miss McClane mentioned that during renovations to the house some funeral urns containing human remains were dug up in the garden. Locally, the house was said to be haunted, but there were no specific details. Apart from the movement of furniture and the mysterious footsteps, Miss McClane had also seen an apparition of the previous owner of the house, standing in the hall and again in the dining-room. 'She appeared quite ordinary,' said Miss McClane.

Another more unusual apparition was seen by Miss McClane as she went from her bedroom to the bathroom. It was the spectre of a tall, well-built man clad in a flowing cloak with a soft brimmed hat on his head. He was referred to jocularly as 'the Sandeman Port man', for that was the image conjured up. He was first seen standing on the landing in a corner, and Miss McClane had to pass him on the way to the bathroom. She had to pass him again on the way back to her room. On further consideration, he appeared to be wearing nineteenth or early twentieth century evening wear. Miss McClane expressed the strong opinion that he resembled a picture she had seen of Sir Roger Casement. She was also of the opinion that 'he' was aware of her, and that some communication passed between them.

After this incident the ladies of the house and their handyman experienced 'the whispering'. The occupants of the house would come into the hall and would hear voices conversing together, but never audible enough to catch the words. This happened most often outside a handsome room known as the Green Room. In the Blue Room, where the handyman occasionally slept, he often encountered an area of freezing cold, as though the room was several degrees below zero. He explained that he would wake in the night to find himself 'frozen' to the point of paralysis. This room was in the older part of the house, up a short flight of stairs, and had the feeling of being a child's room at one time. One had to admire the pragmatic attitude of the handyman, who saw no reason to change rooms, despite the sub-zero temperatures.

As for the bansidhe, both Miss Thompson and Miss McClane had heard the noise separately and together. In one instance the 'keening' seemed to come from a hedge at the bottom of the garden; it terminated in a shriek that raised every hair on their heads.

The second visitation of the bansidhe was even more spectacular. Miss McClane woke suddenly from sleep to hear a low moaning that seemed to be centred in the room itself. This went on for half an hour or so, then the noise became a roar and finished with a truly eldritch shriek. Miss Thompson, who was in the room too, commented, 'Our hair rose on our heads, and I was quite literally too scared to get out of bed. The odd thing was that our two little dogs that slept in the room slept peacefully in their baskets and never stirred.'

When the ladies were questioned at length about the cries, they were both sure that it was like nothing they had heard in their lives before. Yet they both 'knew' what it was; in fact, they found the sobbing quite pitiful and they felt 'sorry for it'. There were one or two unusual aspects to this report of the bansidhe. One was that both women insisted that the sound was inside the room, whereas it is more usual for it to be heard outside, often under a window. The second aspect was that it did not appear to be connected to a death in the house. The ladies did have a sick relative in hospital, but there was nothing to cause anxiety.

There is an unusual postscript to this particular investigation. The author had left her car on the gravel drive at the front of the house, its nose pointing down toward the gate and its near front wheel hard against the grass verge. Upon returning to the car with a companion, the author was surprised to find that the car had executed a sharp right turn onto the lawn at the side of the house and had come to rest only feet from a large greenhouse. It was found that the car was still locked and the handbrake on, so how the car had mounted a substantial verge all by itself was a matter for conjecture. In silence, the car was retrieved and set back onto the drive. The 'joke' had gone far enough for comfort!

The events surrounding Bonamargy Abbey take us back in time from the twentieth century to the eighteenth. The abbey stands just outside Ballycastle on the Coast Road, a favourite place with tourists, not the least for its Lammas Fair held annually in the town centre.

The town takes its name from a castle that once stood on the banks of the Glenshesk River, where the abbey was subsequently raised in 1756. The Bonamargy Abbey, a Franciscan Friary, was founded in 1500 by Rory McQuillan and destroyed in 1504. While the convent itself was small, the church was well proportioned and beautiful. Within its ruins lie the bones of both McQuillans and McDonnells.

Another body lies in Bonamargy, that of Julia McQuillan, better known as 'the Black Nun'. It was here in this quiet spot that this holy woman had her cell, and it was to here that her sister came, one who had sinned grievously, to seek out Julia to hear her confession. Julia, shocked and dismayed by what she had heard of her sister's sins, refused to see her and turned her away. Later her harsh treatment disturbed her, and she was brought to a realization of how cruel her behaviour had been to one seeking aid. Tradition says that a blackbird sang by her window, urging her to 'Let her in, Let her in!'

Julia went in search of her sister and at last saw her a great way off, but as the 'Black Nun' drew near she could see that the woman's face was illuminated by a strange, unearthly light. She fell to her knees beside her sister, realizing, too late, that her sister was dead and bitterly regretting that she, Julia, had shown no compassion or forgiveness. It is said that for the rest of her life she suffered great remorse and performed many penances for her lack of charity to a suffering soul.

Julia also had the gift of prophecy, and men and women came from all over Ireland and beyond to receive her instruction and blessing. In the centuries since then, Julia has been said to walk the abbey. On dark nights, people have heard chanting voices and seen strange lights in the ruins. In the 1940s, one visitor in the late evening saw a woman clad in a long, dark robe walking in the ruined aisle of the church. It was only when the figure glided into a doorway whose exit had long been bricked up that the visitor was forced to assume that he had seen the apparition of Julia, the 'Black Nun'.

At another spot on the coast road with superb views across to the Scottish mainland stands Garron Tower, a nineteenth century castellated building. In the course of the years it has become an educational establishment.

The alleged haunting at Garron Tower is by a former butler, who ended up cutting his own throat. The melancholy creature is seen carrying a basin, in which his severed head lies. On one occasion he forsook his usual haunt and appeared to a local girl at the Black Gate, Nappan, about a mile from his customary walk.

Nappan itself is the haunt of a 'white girl' who was seen by a terrified carter in the last century as he drove his horse and cart home to Glenaan. The horse came to a petrified stop as the girl crossed in front of him and vanished into a wood. Almost at once she re-appeared and stood in front of the cart, so that the driver could see her quite clearly. Throwing his coat over the horse's head and praying as hard as he could, the carter urged the terrified beast past the apparition. The animal fled with such spirit that it didn't stop running until it reached Faavee, three miles up the road. The apparition was reported by several witnesses at various times, and the descriptions tallied very closely. Although this has always been regarded as a genuine paranormal manifestation, no one seems to know who or what 'the white girl' was.

Lisburn is a thriving market town about eleven miles from

Belfast. In earlier times it was at the very heart of the linen industry, and it was very much to the fore during the troubled times of the seventeenth and eighteenth centuries. Fortunately for historical research students, much of its political and cultural history has been recorded, and we can trace the growth of this busy market town.

The name Piper's Hill comes from an old tale about the town in which, during a battle of the seventeenth century, the piper leading the royalist troops had his head blown off by a cannon ball. It was said that his head rolled down one of the narrow lanes in the town centre. Since then the lane has always been known as Piper's Hill, whatever its official designation may be. While Lisburn has a variety of paranormal happenings, a number are clustered about Piper's Hill.

In the 1960s the editor of the local paper, the *Ulster Star*, ran a story on an elderly tenant of one of the cottages on Piper's Hill who had voiced complaints about the cost of rent and rates on what he declared was his haunted cottage. He demanded compensation for his sleepless nights as what he called 'the boots' tramped up and down the stairs at all hours and kept him from his slumbers. The cottage that in fact contained 'the boots' was not his own cottage but the one next door, although it seemed in the dead of night that the party wall did little to mitigate the noise of these ghostly feet.

As was to be expected, the old gentleman received a dusty answer about compensation, but it was while the paper was investigating this story that a great deal more about the paranormal atmosphere on Piper's Hill became known. This time, however, it emanated from the cottage on the other side of 'the boots' cottage, a house occupied by a quiet, respectable family. Next door again lived an elderly woman on her own, who was most derisive about the tales of the boots. At this point the researcher invited by the *Ulster Star* to interview the old gentleman and his neighbours prepared to call it a day and packed up her tape recorder. As she reached the door, the final remark by the old lady stopped her in her tracks. 'Yer man would have something to think on,' said the old woman in belligerent tones, 'if he had the carry-on I have in this cottage with the woman who stands at the fire!' 'What woman?' asked the incredulous researcher. Whereupon the old lady gave her a complete description of the figure of a woman who each evening glided from the back kitchen to stand at the turf fire. She wore a long grey gown and an apron and her head was covered by a cap. She would stand silently by the fire for awhile, and then go back into the kitchen. Since there was no back door, the lady in grey could not escape by any normal means. 'I don't mind her and she don't mind me,' said the old lady. 'And as for that fella next door, why I don't mind his ghosty boots. Sounds like a lot of nonsense!'

The clothes that the apparition was alleged to wear were very reminiscent of the garb worn by the female Huguenot weavers, who had lived in those selfsame cottages two centuries before. These weavers had fled from the Terror in France and had settled as a community in Lisburn to pursue their trade. The cottages that they occupied had one large room downstairs, with a small kitchen or scullery. Below the kitchen, with access by a trap door, was the cellar where the loom was housed. The upper floor was reached by a staircase that led directly from the kitchen, there being no hall or vestibule, while the only door that led to the street was a half-door at the front of the house. Everyone coming or going into the cottage had only one means of entrance or exit via the kitchen.

After the episode of 'the weaver' in cottage 11, it seemed important to investigate the cottage on the other side of the alleged 'haunted boots' cottage, Number 13. The lady of the house was patently nervous and in such evident distress that, upon making enquiries, the editor of the paper found that there were plans afoot by the social services to rehouse her and her family. She was, however, most anxious to tell her story, and as she did the faintly humorous 'tale of the boots' faded into insignificance.

Some weeks before the publicity afforded to Piper's Hill and its ghost, the woman had been preparing dinner, seated by the fire in the kitchen of her home. The children were at school and her husband at work. Suddenly, Mrs McR. heard feet tramping up and down in the bedroom overhead. 'It was a heavy foot, then a light foot,' she explained, 'and the boards creaked back and forth.' She knew there should be no one up there, for she had been at the fire the whole time and no one had passed her. Thinking it might possibly have been one of the children, she called up the stairs. Immediately the noise ceased, only to begin again when she resumed her seat at the fire.

At this point a neighbour arrived for a chat, and in only a little while both women heard the feet upstairs. They went up the stairs a little way and the noise ceased. The neighbour even poked her head in at the bedroom door, but there was nothing and no one there. Directly they returned to the fire, the woman heard the feet again, whereupon the neighbour advised Mrs McR. to go for the priest. Eventually one of the clergy arrived and he examined upstairs and downstairs very thoroughly. Then he suggested that it could have been rats that the women had heard. Mrs McR. was not convinced. 'If it's a rat, Father, then it's a quare big one, in boots!' she told the priest.

Soon none of the family of five would venture upstairs at all. The light in the kitchen stayed on twenty-four hours a day and the family slept downstairs as best they could. The intruder got bolder and smashed windows. Then one afternoon, when the husband ventured to lie down on the bed upstairs, he was hurled bodily to the floor and a heavy plate glass mirror flung out of the window. It is not an exaggeration to say that the family were rapidly being reduced to gibbering wrecks. The police, neighbours and the clergy all kept vigil with the stricken family, to no avail. Eventually the family were evacuated, but not before Mrs McR. had suffered a nervous breakdown.

Once installed in her new home, she was asked by a journalist what she thought 'it' was in the old cottage. She replied with little hesitation, 'It was the noon-day Devil, like we are told about in the Good Book. The noon-day Devil.'

There had always been certain unexplained noises on the hill that, apart from the cottages, only contained a handful of shops: a butcher's, a cobbler's and a small grocery shop. The 'noises' took the form of a woman's light footsteps running down the hill in early evening. Then there were the sounds as of chains being dragged across and up the hill at various times. There were many witnesses who attested to this. All in all, the hill seemed to provoke a great deal of activity. Various theories were put about. One belief was that the public gallows had been situated at the top of the hill, leading into the market square. It was suggested that the condemned men walked up the hill in chains to their deaths and, as the chains were never heard descending the hill, the obvious conclusion was that they would have been taken away in a cart after the execution. It was as good a theory as any.

The episode concerning the particular disturbance at

Number 13 had gone on for about six months and the cottage had lain empty after the family moved out. The cottages in any case were earmarked for demolition, and indeed some were already boarded up so that any further investigation was not possible. Soon the whole row was flattened, and it seemed that another piece of history was to disappear for ever. But that was not quite the case. Such was the reputation of Piper's Hill that few people used it as a short cut after dark; strange incidents continued to be reported. Such an incident occurred in the 1960s, when a woman taking her time walking up the hill in the evening to meet her husband in the market square was met half way up the hill by a truly appalling stench, coupled by a sensation of cold that froze her marrow bones. It seemed to envelope her in its dreadful miasma, and as the victim struggled to the top of the hill she collapsed unconscious and an ambulance had to be called. She told her distressed husband that it seemed as though 'I had walked into another world' and that she felt sure she would suffocate from the dreadful smell of decay. She heard and saw nothing but felt 'people' pressing in on her, whereas in fact the hill was virtually deserted at that time. Some days later, she was asked to point out where the miasma had overtaken her and she identified a part of Piper's Hill, approximately opposite where the door of Number 13 would have stood before being demolished.

A more recent investigation in Lisburn took place in 1990. It was an unusual happening that occurred in a house that had from time to time evinced small paranormal events to the family that lived there. The house had originally been an inn, and the coaches from and to Dublin would have called there. The horses may have been changed here too.

Up to 1990 the incidents in the house had been relatively small and unremarkable: a door swinging open, sounds as though someone was upstairs, or an item in the kitchen displaced. Then, early one Sunday morning, all that changed. It should be said, perhaps, that over the years some modifications had taken place in the house, but it was largely as it had been built – namely, a comfortable farmhouse with a commodious stable yard. The house had been almost continuously occupied during its lifetime.

Early on Sunday morning, 18 November 1990, Mr X went downstairs to the sitting-room with its adjoining conservatory to find, scattered on the floor, the following items: a carriage clock from the centre of the mantlepiece (undamaged) and a large framed picture of the Serengeti that usually hung over the mantlepiece. It had a small dent, and now it lay face up some distance from the clock, on the carpet. Its hanging cord was undamaged and the nails on which it had hung were still in the wall. A row of valuable figurines, strung out along the mantlepiece in front of the picture and on either side of the clock, were completely untouched.

The first question a rather baffled Mr X had to ask himself was how had the picture managed to 'hop' over the figurines and lay itself face up on the floor, without anything being shattered. Later he was to discover a Staffordshire figure that had stood at the far end of the mantlepiece, lying upside down but undamaged in the log basket which stood at the far end of the fireplace.

Nothing else was missing or even disturbed. The supposed gyrations of clock and picture would have involved hopping and jumping off a mantle shelf a good foot wide and made of solid marble. A picture falling off a wall for no apparent reason has, in many areas of the British isles, always been regarded as a death warning. Thus, despite their sound common sense in the matter, the owners were a trifle apprehensive. As it happened a previous owner, an elderly woman, did die the next day, so there may or may not have been a connection.

When Mrs X was asked if anything else of note had happened in the house, she thought for a moment and then mentioned two other incidents. On the Saturday night before the 'jumping picture' episode, the door of a small cloakroom in the hall suddenly slammed shut, despite the fact that it was notoriously stiff and not in a location that might have rendered it vulnerable to a sudden draught. It had, she thought, behaved in a similar fashion on another occasion. The other incident was a great deal stranger. One night after a dinner party Mrs X had washed up and dried the dinner service and stacked it on the Welsh dresser in the kitchen prior to putting it away. She decided that, as it was quite late, she would put the plates and other items away in the morning, and consequently went off to bed. When she came down to the kitchen in the morning, she found the dishes still neatly stacked – but now they were reposing on the floor instead of the dresser! In answer to the query as to whether she had heard anything during the night, the answer was no.

When one delved into the history of the house, the only faintly sinister detail to emerge was that some thirty to forty years earlier there had been the tragic murder of a young woman, attacked by a young man of her acquaintance. The question then arose: was the disturbance to the picture some form of poltergeist manifestation with connections to the forthcoming death of the previous owner of the house, or had it to do with the earlier violent death in the house? One might also have wondered if any member of the family possessed some quality of kinetic energy that might have been a trigger. As far as is ascertainable, there have been no other incidents in the last three years.

9   Bansidhe

County Antrim is quite fruitful ground for learning more about the 'bansidhe' or 'fairy woman'. A number of the Ulster bansidhe are 'roe' or 'redhaired', and it may be recalled that one of the races from which the Irish sprang was the Goidelic Celt, who were predominately red-haired. One often asks what exactly a bansidhe might be. Many years ago an elderly man in Antrim proferred this explanation: 'Just as we all have a guardian angel, so do the Irish tribes or families have an angel to watch over them. But angelic beings were not normally capable of feeling joy or sorrow, such as we mortals feel. So the Lord God relented, and allowed the tribal angel to express grief at the passing of one of her human family. That's why the bansidhe cries.'

Another theory is that the bansidhe is an inherited memory, and just as we inherit red hair or blue eyes so we inherit a tribal memory of a woman weeping over her dead. In the troubled land of Ireland, this image must have always been a fairly common experience. So perhaps 'the memory' comes as a four minute warning before a tragic event and it is a level of our subliminal consciousness that releases it.

Most of the great families of the chiefs and High Kings were followed by the 'fairy woman', although she could manifest in various guises. Some families are followed by black birds that come and cry before a death; one or two are followed by a butterfly or a phantom tree. One family, the O Neill chiefs, had one of their own kin as bansidhe. The story goes that an O Neill chief on his way to help his neighbour, the Maquillans, found when he arrived at the meeting place a milk white heifer caught in a thorn tree by the horns. In order to release her, O Neill had to chop a branch off the tree. Unfortunately the tree was a fairy thorn, and to damage fairy property was very ill luck. As it transpired, after O Neill assisted his neighbour he returned home to find that the fairies had stolen away his daughter Kathleen as a punishment. Kathleen was allowed home now and then, and she would often come to 'keen' for the family at a death. She became, in effect, the O Neill bansidhe.

As tradition dictates, Kathleen had her own room in the castle. In warning of a death she would have worn her shawl over her head, but at joyful times, such as weddings or christenings, she would be seen with the shawl about her shoulders. Some of the castle servants maintained that, after she had called, they would see an imprint on the bed in her chamber. She was a 'bansidhe roe'. This tradition supports one of the theories that bansidhe are human spirits, doomed to play this role after death, or that the fairies have some dealings in the matter, probably as in the O Neill case – for revenge.

The descriptions and variations of the bansidhe tradition span the centuries from the dawn of Irish history to the cry of the bansidhe in a Belfast street in the twentieth century. In *Visions and Beliefs in the West of Ireland* by Lady Gregory, a notable folklorist of the nineteenth century, the bansidhe of the great warrior Cuchulain was described thus:

Then Cuchulain went his way, and Cathbad that followed him went with him. And presently they came to a ford and there was a young girl, thin and white skinned and having yellow hair, washing and ever washing, and wringing out clothing that was stained crimson red, keening all the time. 'Little Hound,' said Cathbad, 'do you see what that young girl is doing? It is your red clothes she is washing, and crying as she washes, because she knows that you are going to your death against Maeve's great army ...

This scene dissolves into a Belfast street on a cold winter's night in the 1970s. A young man is coming on a late night shift in the local bakery, along with a group of workmates. He has scarcely been working at the vans' loading bays for twenty minutes when a low moaning sound is heard in the yard. One or two men stop to listen, then one shrugs his shoulders. 'Them old cats!', he mutters, but his companion is uneasily silent.

The sound grows and contains an element of humanity, a sobbing and a shriller note of grief and pain. It comes and goes, but gradually the men stop work and gather together in the doorway of the bakehouse. No one seems anxious to investigate, until the young man who was the last to arrive at work notes that the noise seems to come from beside where his own van is parked. He strolls towards it, hesitantly, but as he approaches the sound fades and almost dies away. After a moment he turns to rejoin his workmates. Again, the sound revives until it becomes a thin, high wail that carries within it all the sorrows of the world.

One of the older men takes off his cap and blesses himself surreptitiously. 'I'm not liking this,' he mutters, and retreats inside the bakery. The headlights of a car swing in an arc as a vehicle drives into the yard. It stops, and a young boy in a duffle coat runs across to the men.

'Where's our Tommy?' he asks. 'Our Tommy! He must come away home!' There is doom in his voice, and the young van-man steps forward.

'Yes, I'm here! Sammy, what's wrong?' A few hurried words in what is now a deep and dreadful silence. Then he gets into the car with the boy, and they are driven away.

The other men look at each other while one who was nearer to the car than the rest says, 'It's the mother.... The wee lad's mother's been took bad.' They stare after the car and then turn to stare at the van from where the 'calling' had come.

'I never believed in them old tales,' said the man with the cap, who had returned to join the others in the yard. 'I never knew Tommy's family was "followed" by one of "them". My auntie heard her once, so she said anyway, just before my father died. You never forget the sound they say – never!' He closed his eyes and repeated something. Nobody called 'her' by her rightful name.

Further up the Antrim Coast Road towards Bushmills and the Giant's Causeway lies Dunluce Castle, a spectacular ruin on the cliff's edge looking seaward. Many centuries ago the lord of the castle possessed a beautiful daughter, who had just attained her seventeenth year. She was a gentle child, both loving and good, and she was well thought of for her generosity and charity towards those in need. She spent a great deal of her time walking around her father's estate, caring for the wants of the poor and needy. During her walks she chanced upon a young man and, in due time, the young couple fell hopelessly in love. One has to say 'hopelessly', for she was bound to her father's choice of a husband in an arranged marriage. She determined that she could not wed where she did not love, and that death would be preferable. So, sadly, she sat in her chamber and wove herself a shroud.

When her father asked her what she was doing she told him. 'I am making my shroud, father.' The father, who had assumed that she was working at her bridal gown, was both alarmed and angry. With further questioning he soon found out about her love affair. He told her she was a disobedient daughter, and that she would stay in her room until she changed her mind. 'We'll see if you will disobey me!' he warned her.

Every day he asked the same question and received the same answer – that she was 'making her shroud'. Soon he saw that the shroud was nearly finished, and that his punishment had had little effect. He made enquiries about her lover, to find that he was a noble youth of good character and quite suitable to wed his daughter. Yet he could not lose face by relenting, and so he cast about for a way of saving her life and retaining his own authority at the same time.

One wild and stormy day, when her father was away from home, the girl found to her surprise that her prison was unlocked, and one of her father's servants told her that her lover waited below. The servant eagerly took the gold she offered and said he would help the couple escape. Sure enough, a small boat was fortuitously to hand and the young couple ran to it and prepared to sail away.

Unknown to his daughter, the father watched the 'escape' from another window in the castle, for it was he who had planned it all. In due time, faced with a fait accompli, he would forgive the young pair and thus restore his daughter to favour, without sacrificing his pride. Then, to his horror, he saw a freak wave strike the tiny boat and his daughter disappear into the water. A second later another wave overturned the boat, and there was no one left. Alas, his love and care for his daughter, tainted by his overwhelming pride, had brought about her tragic death. The father fell down unconscious from grief.

For weeks he walked the shoreline, wringing his hands and crying out for his daughter until it was believed he would go mad. Sometimes he would sit and look up at her window in the tower and sigh bitterly. Then one day a vision of his daughter appeared and he could see her in her room, wearing her shroud and carrying the broom with which, daily during her imprisonment, she had swept her chamber. 'How long? How long?', the distraught father cried to the apparition. 'For ever, Father,' came her faint reply. 'For ever.'

Thus it was that the lovely and tragic Maeve became the family bansidhe and appeared sweeping her chamber when the family was to have bad news. Eventually the family died out, and Maeve came no longer to weep at Dunluce Castle. But on a clear, still night one can still hear the sound of sweet singing and the noise and rustle of a broom from Maeve's room.

Returning to the city of Belfast, in October, 1938, a Mrs English, who lived in the Castleton Gardens area of Belfast, was walking beside the railing of Alexandra Park one afternoon. She was alone on the road until she saw someone coming out of Jubilee Avenue from the direction of the Antrim Road.

As Mrs English watched, the woman crossed the road and went into the park, where she could be seen clearly on the main path. Suddenly, the figure disappeared, and when Mrs English got to the gates she saw that they were locked.

According to Mrs English, the event took place at about five o'clock, and the woman had been wearing a black shawl with what looked like a long white skirt underneath. The witness recalled that this was the typical garb worn by the nineteenth century spinners who would have worked in the mill nearby. Somewhat shocked, the witness had to conclude that the figure she had seen was apparitional. The woman had gone into the park through locked gates, and then she had disappeared in the middle of a clearly defined path with no cover on either side. 'The woman was visible to me all the time,' Mrs English maintained.

In over a quarter of a century of personal investigation, the author has noted that a majority of poltergeist events have happened in the city of Belfast itself. This makes sense, for logic decrees that one would hear of a number of cases proportionate to the number of people in an area, because poltergeist manifestation does imply 'haunted people' more than 'haunted places'. A manifestation may happen in a very small way for a short space of time. An example of this is the case of a lone lady teacher who, on moving to a terraced house in the south end of the city, for nearly three months was treated to a small but embarrassing assault on her person every time she came home from work. The emphatic 'pinch' happened in the hallway of her home as she closed the door. After about twelve weeks, the pinching stopped, to the lady's intense relief! Alternatively, there have been a number of cases where the activity was prolonged and seemed to increase in intensity. In most cases, it was extremely unpleasant. The Piper's Hill case in Lisburn has already been cited, and many others of a similar nature have occurred.

It is quite difficult at times to disentangle poltergeist phenomena which appears not to be associated with a specific personality from that which, on closer examination, seems to be connected with an event that may have taken place in the house and may attach itself more to one particular person.

In the late 1960s, in response to a telephone call, two investigators were dispatched to the north of the city to interview an English couple who had just settled in Northern Ireland from the north of England. They were a young middle-aged couple with two children. At first, all went well. They were pleased with the house, the locale and the facilities provided. Mrs R. stayed at home while Mr R., an engineer, worked in the shipyard. After less than a month Mrs R. began to feel that, once the family had gone out, she was not alone in the house. She sensed 'someone' following her about, and once she felt pressure, like a hand, on her shoulder.

Starting from this indefinable sense of another person, there was increasing activity in the house. Items were moved about in the kitchen, in particular in the food cupboards. The electric lights behaved in a bizarre fashion; tumbler switches clicked themselves on and off, the door chimes rang with no one at the door and, despite Mr R.'s minute examination of switches and circuitry, there was nothing to be found.

Then the children complained of a shadowy figure in their bedroom, and said they could hear their names called, as could Mrs R.

After bearing with this for about a month, Mrs R. made contact with the researchers, who went to see her. The first thing they noted was that Mrs R. referred to the disturbing entity as 'her'. When questioned, she said she was convinced the presence she felt was female. While the researchers were present, they both heard knocking at the front door, as did Mr R. Mrs R. did not seem to react to this, but a few moments later she became quite agitated and told the researchers that she felt 'it' near, and it was patently obvious that she was very frightened indeed.

An examination of the area showed that the new house in which Mr and Mrs R. lived had been built on land that had once contained a very old house. But on further enquiry it seemed that nothing unusual had happened there. There were no reports of crimes of violence or any other tragedy. In the interval of about ten days between the first and second visits to the house, the poltergeist manifestations continued. Items in the kitchen moved about, inexplicable pools of water appeared, and the electricity system went 'haywire'. Finally the researchers returned together with a 'sensitive' who, although not a professional medium, had had some success in the past with contacting discarnate entities.

The entity now called Mrs R. by her Christian name, 'Mary', and once or twice Mrs R. heard a voice asking her to 'pray for me'. After a long and tiring session with the sensitive, the entity calling herself 'May' communicated via the medium, and a sad and sorry tale was revealed. 'May' had lived in the old house and had been a dutiful, if fearful, daughter of an old man who was both eccentric and unbending. Eventually the old man died, and within a short time 'May' died as well. She had hated and feared her father, and she was horribly afraid that after death he would continue to dominate her.

This, it seemed, was why she had remained, for want of a better word, 'earthbound' in an attempt to stay out of her father's clutches. She had become a lonely and frightened soul, and in Mrs R. she had sensed a sympathy and understanding that she had never received in life. She had not meant to frighten the family, only to attempt to communicate with them. Finally 'May' was persuaded to leave Mrs R. alone and, in turn, prayers were offered for her. Mrs R. made it abundantly clear that she did not want 'May' harmed in any way, and certainly she did not wish the house to be exorcised.

'May' ceased her activities, and some months later the R. family went back to England. It was touching to see that, despite her own doubts and fears, Mrs R. had been compassionate in very trying circumstances, and in that must be a lesson for all of us. The house evidently reverted to total normality after the R.s' departure.

The case of the unhappy 'May' was a relatively small episode of poltergeist activity compared to one investigated in February, 1989, in a three-storey terrace house, again in the north of the city. The house was newly occupied by a father, mother and two small children under the age of four. The haunting of the house consisted of a sustained series of poltergeist events. The house was of sturdy brick construction and was built about 1910. There had been some disturbance in the house prior to the new owners coming, for the previous owner had complained of thumps, bumps and knockings in the two attic rooms, and of doors opening and closing on their own. When the Osbornes arrived, they too complained of activity, not only in the attics but in the bedroom on the next floor and, at infrequent intervals, on the stairs and in the rest of the house.

Apart from knocks and bangs, the electricity was extensively interfered with. There were short circuiting incidents, the doorbell rang frequently, items of household use became 'electrified' with plugs jumping out of their sockets, and trails of sparks passed from one electrical appliance to another. The electricity service was called but could find no explanation for the 'wild' electricity.

Other events occurred, including Mr Osborne's name being called, and one of the children being slapped violently about the face, the slap leaving an imprint of fingers on the child's face. Mrs Osborne saw 'something white' floating above the children's cots. Then one of the children's coats was reduced to rags, as though it had been soaked in acid, and two apparitions were seen on the stairs and in one of the bedrooms. One apparition was of a large man, the other of a little girl.

The incidents became so bad that Mrs Osborne, now heavily pregnant with her third child, refused to go upstairs at all when alone in the house, even to use the bathroom. Consequently Mr Osborne now had to stay home from work. A Christian group moved in to help, and the family also had help from a professional medium. For awhile the manifestations grew less. Then, in the New Year 1990, they surged again and matters became very bad indeed. At this point, with a new baby, the family was at the end of its tether and moved out.

Despite intensive enquiries, nothing conclusive came to light about the house. The history of the disturbances only spanned ten years of the eighty-year-old house. However, there were one or two points of interest. One was the fact that, despite the assurance of neighbours that nothing had happened in the house prior to the present disturbances, it had stood empty at fairly frequent intervals over the years, and this in an area always in demand for housing. In addition, one night a neighbour had been 'attacked' by something in her own house, and she had a badly scratched face to prove it. She mentioned also that at one time there had been 'a bad tempered child' next door, who was seldom seen outside. The case of the child's coat being burnt was investigated, and the analysis showed that some fluid akin to battery acid had been used. The electricity problems were never explained, even when they got to the stage where whole areas of the house became 'live', and by touching one another the family could provoke showers of sparks.

While there was no satisfactory conclusion to this affair, one does have to bear in mind that there were two small children in the house, whom even their mother described as hyper-active. Although this may have had some bearing on the amount of pure energy released in the house, it is at best only a conjecture. The good news was that, on moving out of the area, the family had no further problems. At least not of a poltergeistic nature.

To end this discussion of poltergeist manifestations, another case attracted attention barely six months after the last, but in the west side of Belfast. Again, it involved a family with children, ranging this time from five to fifteen. This case became well known locally as 'The Woman in Black' and attracted quite a lot of media and press attention. The location again was a small modern terrace house, built on the site of older buildings. The 'radiant centre' of this manifestation appeared to be the father of the family, who in the weeks that followed was assaulted at times so violently that it necessitated the family forsaking their home and going to stay with friends and neighbours for safekeeping. In the course of the disturbance water taps, lights, the doors and the furniture were interfered with, together with apparitional sightings and changes of temperature.

The most unpleasant of the phenomena which appeared to the man of the house and at times, to the eldest son, was 'The Woman in Black' – an apparition of a young woman dressed all in black and with a faintly Victorian air about her. This woman seemed to be particularly hostile towards the husband, and he was subjected to beatings, being thrown over the banisters and knocked down the stairs. The entity took strong objection to certain items left in the house by the clergy and concerned neighbours. These included candles that had been blessed, rosaries and crucifixes.

After some of the more physically violent episodes, it became necessary for John S. and his wife to have protection from stouthearted friends on a twenty-four hour basis until they quit the house. The apparition resisted any attempt to remove her, despite clerical intervention and a vigil being kept in the street by their Catholic neighbours. Mass was said in the house, and the celebrant himself could vouch for the sense of a hostile presence. Some of the neighbours began to fear for the sanctity of their own homes, as the disturbances began to spill over to neighbours on either side. The family's belongings that remained in the house were frequently broken and destroyed.

It was imperative that the children be removed from this scene of violence, and in fact it would be difficult to assess how much trauma was suffered by them, not only from the psycho-kinetic energy expended but from the loss of their own home and separation, however temporary, from their parents. Several paranormalists investigated the site, but no conclusions were drawn. Even when the furore had died down and the house lay vacant, there was no guarantee that the manifestations had ceased. Understandably, it was some time before a tenant could be found to take on such a notorious dwelling. It may be that the phenomenon was linked only to the family of John S., as does occur in cases of this kind, and there seemed to be no history of disturbance before the family went to live in the house. Presumably, only time will tell if 'The Woman in Black' was a one-off event.

Outside the city boundaries, on the River Lagan in County Antrim, lies the small village of Lambeg or Llann Bheag: Little Church. It is a village that was mentioned in the Domesday Book and stands in the heartland of the linen industry. It had been a monastic site from before 1590, when it was home to the Franciscan Order. The church now standing in the village dates from 1598, while within the village itself can be seen the former site of the nunnery, hospice for travellers, and the community burial grounds. There once was a fine house standing in the village, known locally as 'The Chains' but officially as Lambeg House. King William stopped here on his way to the Boyne and sheltered under a magnificent chestnut tree. The house, alas, is no more, a victim of latter day violence. Where it once stood is a small memorial park.

Lambeg's most famous inhabitant, however, still makes an occasional foray on to the main street and up the winding hill to the church. The slender and mysterious figure of the 'Grey Lady of Lambeg' has been seen often in the centuries that separate her time from ours.

She is believed to be the apparition of one of that early community of sisters who had Lambeg as their home and tended the poor and needy, as well as the traveller in the hospice of early times. The sisters are remembered best by the 'Nun's Garden', an ancient burial site at the rear of the church. It is near the garden that the Grey Lady is most often seen. She may also be seen walking along the road from the village to the church gates. There is no specific tale about her, and we do not know her name or her history. Yet many a traveller taking his time up the hill has been joined by a shadowy figure who, despite his attempts to quicken his step, has no difficulty in keeping pace with him until, at the lych gate, she vanishes. There was a report in the 1970s that she or another 'lady' had been seen in one of the church cottages, appearing on the stairs and holding a book. Outside another house in Sandy Lane, about a quarter of a mile away, the figure of a nun has been seen looking out of an upstairs window of an old house, appearing to be standing on the floor level that would have been there in her time. In the road outside this house the figure has also been seen in the lower branches of a tree, although what the good sister was doing up a tree is problematical! We cannot, of course, say that all these sightings were of the Grey Lady herself.

In the 1970s a new bungalow estate was built on the site of the old hospice, and at least one householder heard footsteps in and around his bungalow. On one occasion a man's form materialized briefly in his sitting-room against the curtains. The young son, a boy of eight, had seen a man in his bedroom – a stranger, the child said, 'with a sad face' who vanished by way of the window. The child did not seem to be anxious about his visitor and informed his parents that the man was a regular visitor.

In the 1960s and 1970s the Grey Lady was quite a regular visitor, and hardly a week went by when someone didn't see her. After that she became a less frequent figure on the road, but as late as 1986 a taxi driver waiting in the church car park to drive an elderly worshipper home from church saw her leaning on a gravestone and looking, according to the bemused witness, 'very solid'. Then she melted away. Of late, there have been no reports of her.

Although the following story from Lambeg is not strictly a paranormal one, nevertheless it has a tragic and mysterious quality that makes it worth the telling. It is the story of Essy Pelan, whose grave lies next to the Nun's Garden. Her grave is surrounded by an iron railing and has a beautiful memorial inscription dating from the early nineteenth century. Essy had lived in the village all her life, working, as did most of her friends, at the linen trade. Essy had a sweetheart, and while he loved Essy dearly they had no money to wed. After much discussion, the young man decided that he would go to America where he could make some money. When he sorted out his problems, he would send for Essy.

A year passed, and information from or about her sweetheart was very scarce. Essy grew despondent and lonely. Sometimes, if someone came back from America, they might bring a scrap of news, or a brief scrawled letter might arrive. Spiteful tongues in the village hinted that he might have found himself someone new and forgotten about Essy. Then, over a particularly hard winter, Essy fell ill, perhaps with consumption. As her grieving family watched, Essy faded away before their eyes, and still no word came. She was only twenty-one when they closed her eyes for the last time. They dressed her in her wedding gown that Essy had sewn so carefully against the time when she would be a bride, and on her hair they laid a wreath of myrtle and white roses.

Essy was carried up the hill to the church and into the old churchyard beside the Nun's Garden, and there they laid her to rest. But there was worse to come. As they laid her in the earth, her sweetheart arrived home unexpectedly. He had secured a good job and now had come to take Essy back to America with him. Sadly, Essy's parents led him, weeping, to her grave. That grave can still be seen, as can the words that the distraught young man caused to be inscribed on the grey stone above Essy's head:

Died on the Anniversary of her birthday,
1 March 1833, aged twenty-one years.
Separated below ... United above.
I weep the more because I weep in vain
Thou wert my life
The ocean to the river of my thoughts
Which terminated all

10   The Voice from the Dead

This seventeenth century account of a very unusual haunting comes from Drumbeg, County Down. In those days the area was known as Drumbridge, as the road passed over the River Lagan. The time is the autumn of 1662. One Francis Taverner, a servant of Lord Chichester, was riding homeward from Hillsborough to Mallon (Malone), County Antrim. Mallon is now on the edge of what can be called Greater Belfast, on the south side of the city.

Suddenly, there appeared on the road beside Taverner an apparition in a white robe and on horseback, with two other riders beside him. The apparition bore a resemblance to James Haddock, whom Taverner had known slightly in life and whose remains now lay in the churchyard at Drumbeg; the wall that Taverner was passing belonged to that churchyard. It is believed that Haddock died about 1657. The apparition identified itself to Taverner by recalling some trivial incident that had taken place in Taverner's father's house, while Haddock was still alive. The apparition became increasingly agitated and begged Taverner to ride with him, as he had a favour to ask. Understandably, the terrified Taverner clapped spurs to his horse and fled, while from behind him came the sound of a 'mighty wind' and other violent noises that scared him out of his wits.

After a week or so, as the memory of the ghastly encounter began to fade, Taverner assumed that the visitation was unlikely to be repeated and he regained his customary good humour. However once more the apparition appeared before him, this time at his own fireside, begging most piteously that Taverner would give him aid. Partly through fright and partly through pity, Taverner agreed to listen to Haddock's story.

The ghost complained that, after his death, his widow,

Eleanor Walsh, had married a man called Davis. Davis had known Haddock all his life, and was in fact one of the executor's of Haddock's will. This duty included guarding the rights of Haddock's young son, David, until he came of age. Davis, however, had abused that trust with regard to some property and had defrauded the boy. Haddock now wanted the matter to be laid before the justices, and this was the 'aid' that he required of Taverner – to act, as it were, 'in loco parentis'.

Despite the pity that Francis Taverner felt for the apparition, he was loathe to get mixed up in Haddock's affairs, especially if Davis was involved – a man notorious for his violent ways. Taverner was also a logical man, and could see no reason why anyone should believe this bizarre tale. He protested that, much as he would like to, he really could not help. Then the apparition fell into a terrible rage and told Taverner that 'he would have no peace', a threat it proceeded to carry out by tormenting Taverner night and day with music, yells and bangs, and hammering on the furniture. The crowning terror was when Francis woke in the night and found Haddock bending over him, threatening to choke him if Taverner did not contact Eleanor Walsh at once. With the threats of being 'torn to pieces' ringing in his ears, Taverner confided his plight to Lord Chichester's chaplain, a man called James South, who advised him to carry out the apparition's wishes, such requests from the departed being regarded as sacrosanct in those days.

For some days after seeking out Haddock's widow, Taverner had peace. Then Haddock came again, and this time demanded that Taverner inform the executors, and these, of course, included Davis, that he was to make a complaint. When the terrified Taverner pointed out that to tell Davis was more than his life was worth, the apparition promised, somewhat vaguely, to protect him and put the fear of God into Davis. By now Taverner was so beside himself with anxiety that he sought advice from no less a person than the great divine Bishop Jeremy Taylor, who presided over the diocesan court of Down. The bishop, however, was more interested in eliciting spiritual information from the apparition than concerning himself unduly with Taverner's plight. He required Taverner to question the apparition, asking such questions as: 'Whence came you?' and 'Where is your abode?', which the apparition refused to answer. Furthermore, that same night, as Taverner rested at the house of Lord Conway, the apparition crawled over the wall and manifested itself to several people.

One ray of hope for Taverner was that the worthy bishop decided to take up the case and bring it to court. Naturally, the apparition was delighted and assured Taverner of signs and wonders to back up his story. One of these 'wonders' was that the grave slab on Haddock's tomb refused to lie straight, no matter how often it was put right. This was meant to be a token of the 'crooked dealings' that Haddock had had to suffer. It is true that if one visits the grave the stone is turned at a curious angle against the general inclination of the surrounding ground, despite efforts to rectify this.

At last the case came to the church court in Carrickfergus, presided over by Bishop Taylor. Meanwhile, Davis had hired a clever attorney, who intended to get Taverner laughed out of court. Taverner realized, gloomily, what a figure of fun he was, and that as sole witness to this extraordinary complaint his evidence would be untenable. Having set the court sniggering at some witticism, the attorney for Davis enquired sarcastically if Taverner wished to call a witness. Taverner, now at the end of his patience, appealed to the bishop. 'Call James Haddock!'

There was uproar in the court, but after momentary hesitation the bishop, determined to show justice being done, instructed the court usher to do just that: 'Call James Haddock!' Bishop Taylor said gravely to the court, 'I must allow it, for assuredly this man is known unto God, whose servant I am.'

'James Haddock, come into the court!' the usher called out three times. On the third call there was a clap of thunder and a man's hand was seen on the table of the clerk of the court while a voice demanded, 'Is this enough?'

It seemed that it was, both for the bishop and the hushed courtroom. The case was accepted and matters set in motion for Davis' affairs to be looked into.

It is said that Davis rode away from court swearing all kinds of vengeance on Francis Taverner, and matters might have faired ill for him if, on the way home past the Drumbridge churchyard, Davis' horse had not taken fright at 'something' in the road and thrown him to the ground, breaking his neck. Five years later a man called Costlett, who had aided and abetted Davis, also died from a fall from his horse, in approximately the same spot.

There appear to be some grounds for this unusual tale,

based on historical fact. The bishop's secretary at that time was Thomas Alcott, who set down details of the case in a letter, and certainly there was an account set down by Joseph Glanville, Chaplain-in-Ordinary to Charles II. There were minor variations, but in the main the story remained the same.

There is a postscript. In the autumn of 1973, the author received a call from an elderly lady who, passing by the church at Drumbeg in the early evening, saw a man's head bobbing up and down inside the old churchyard wall. 'He appeared to be trotting on a horse,' she explained. 'He wore a coat with a tall collar.' She did not stay to investigate further but fled to the safety of her car. It is interesting to note that the front wall of Drumbeg Church today would approximate to the location of the road from Drumbridge to Mallon that had been frequented by both Taverner and Haddock. This witness was quite convinced that she had seen James Haddock, whose body lay beyond the wall.

Down Patrick (Dun Padraig: St Patrick's Fort) is an ancient and interesting town standing near where the widening River Quoile enters Strangford Lough. Here in the churchyard of the Church of Ireland Cathedral is an enormous block of granite that traditionally covers St Patrick's grave. In fact the old rhyme says: 'Three saints one grave do fill, Patrick, Brigid and Columcille.'

Near to Down is the little townland of Saul, a site given by the chieftain Dichu for Patrick to build his first church. Outside the town is a stretch of road haunted, it is said, by an old woman in a shawl and a phantom coach. Three Mile Hill is haunted by two children, believed to be famine victims. And then there are the gates of Finnebrogue House.

These famous gates once adorned the chief entrance to the house, not far from Inch Abbey on the banks of the Quoile. All that may be seen of them now are two crumbling stone pillars standing behind the present wall of the demesne. The present entrance to the house has been moved a few yards down the road, leaving the gates to stand alone amid a tangle of shrub and weed.

Local legend has it that the stones used to make the gates were taken from the ruined abbey of Inch, and from the moment that the gates were hung on the pillar stones things started to go wrong. The first curious event was that the gates refused to hang properly. Workmen would erect them one day and the next day would find them lying on the ground. Keeping guard to watch for the culprits responsible proved fruitless, for under the astonished eyes of watchers the gates detached themselves!

Trying to persuade horses to pass through them was a wasted effort, and many a gentleman had to dismount and throw his coat over his horse's head in order to walk the frightened animal through the gates. Eventually, the masters of Finnebrogue House bowed to the unknown power and the gates were abandoned and a new entrance built. The fact that the stone had come from a sanctified spot was cited by local people as the reason for these strange disturbances.

A more recent report surfaced on an event that took place at Inch Abbey itself. Inch was founded in 1187 by John De Courcy, a Norman knight, on the site of an older Celtic monastery. It was occupied, at De Courcy's behest, by monks from Furness Abbey in Yorkshire. Here in this beautiful and tranquil spot on the river bank the Cistercian community cultivated its land and tended its flocks in one of the most revered sites in Ireland. For many years they spent their days in prayer and thanksgiving, until the dark days came and the abbey lay desolate. Yet there is still a sense of peace and tranquillity among its ancient stones.

In the late summer of 1980 two visitors were strolling about the abbey ruins and enjoying the sights and sounds of the river, occasionally stopping to look across the fields to where the spire of Down Cathedral could be seen. The husband, a keen photographer, was taking shots of the ruins and was standing with his back to the river to get a good angle; his wife was standing at the water's edge, admiring a family of swans. While she watched the swans, a small boat came round the curve of the bank, and on board were three men. They were sailing about one hundred yards off shore; two of the men were seated while the third, half standing in the stern, was trailing a piece of rope in the water. The boat appeared to be drifting with a prevailing current.

The wife watched the boat idly as it crossed her line of vision and then sailed gently around the edge of a small grassy island. She found herself speculating on what the men were doing and, turning, tried to catch her husband's attention. 'I wonder what they're fishing for?' she queried. 'They seem a bit close in.'

'Who's a bit close in?' asked her husband, giving the river a cursory glance.

'The men in the boat, of course!' responded the wife with an exasperated edge to her voice. Her husband looked mystified. 'What boat? What men? What on earth are you talking about?'

She could see the tail end of the boat just disappearing out of sight behind a grassy headland. The wife gave a snort of disbelief. 'Have you gone blind, or what? That boat over there!'

'I can't see a boat,' replied her husband, a trifle nettled by her tone. 'There's no boat or men. I can only see the river.'

Without replying the wife hurried along the river bank to a vantage point where she was bound to see the boat emerging from around the headland. But the river was empty; no boat, no men. Nothing.

Ahead of the woman two elderly men were strolling along the river bank. The woman ran up to them. 'I'm sorry for troubling you,' she said, 'but can you tell me, did you notice a small boat a moment ago, out there?' And she indicated the spot where she had first seen it. The men looked puzzled. 'A boat? What boat, we never saw any.' 'I can't have imagined it,' the woman blurted out. 'It was real, solid and so were the men!' She described what she had seen and added, 'They were dressed in sort of greyish woollen jersey. I could see that they nearly reached their knees. One was standing up, he had a rope in his hand, while the other two were sitting down. I thought they were fishing.' The older of the two men looked at her a trifle oddly and said, 'Ah well now, maybe it was the brothers you saw fishing. A wee bit of fish for the supper, likely.' He smilingly refused to elucidate further but winked at his companion. The man and his wife turned away, still confused at what the woman had seen.

Some months later the same couple were attending a meeting on local folklore, when they got into conversation with the speaker for the evening and they told her about the 'three men in a boat'. She became quite excited.

'How extraordinary!' she declared. 'You are not going to believe this, but I had an almost identical experience at Inch. I saw a boat with three men in it that I took to be fishing. Just like you, I drew my husband's attention to it, only for him to say "What boat!" I knew he wasn't pulling my leg. He really could not see it.'

The two women began to confirm details about the men's

clothes, and the lecturer suggested that what they had thought were 'jerseys' could have been the top half of cassocks, and the 'rope' in one of the men's hands could have been a girdle. Neither woman had heard any noises from the boat and it had had no distinguishing features.

The interesting slant on this event was that this was a perfect example of someone experiencing an event which, had they not mentioned it to another person, they might never have known that they were seeing an apparition. It makes it doubly interesting that another person could confirm the sighting and gives added weight to the view that many people will declare that they have never had a paranormal experience simply because the experience was so 'normal' that they would not have had any reason to question it. One wonders how many other visitors to Inch Abbey had seen 'the three men in a boat' on other occasions.

One of the most popular of tourist venues in County Down is the town of Newcastle, situated picturesquely where the 'Mountains of Mourne sweep down to the sea'. It has a fine strand and a sturdy fishing fleet, although its main industry is tourism.

Newcastle Harbour is the site for a bansidhe, and over the course of two centuries she has been heard near the harbour walk. The basis of her grief is said to be that of the loss of her lover during a bad winter storm. She is most frequently seen by those recently bereaved themselves.

A second apparition is that of a woman riding a jet black horse in the very late hours. She favours the north promenade on a fine moonlit night. The third haunting takes the form of an old fisherman in dark jersey and seaboots who sometimes sits by the harbour wall, gazing out to sea. It is said that he foretells a storm. Last but not least, Newcastle has its own 'black dog' who frequents the shore in front of Newcastle's most prestigious hotel, the Slieve Donard. Obviously a hound with a taste for the high life!

One associates hotels with the quiet clinking of glasses and the hum of conversation in the bar. While the Slieve Donard has no history of the paranormal, there is a bar in nearby Holywood, County Down, that had quite a lively 'visitor'. Chiccarinos Bar was a popular and thriving restaurant, but it had inherited a poltergeist along with the bar room fitting. Both management and guests would hear voices and noise coming from rooms that were unoccupied. Some mornings bottles would be found half-empty, and yet the bar staff could swear to cleaning up the bar thoroughly the night before. This practice extended more worryingly to the kitchens and the gas appliances, which were sometimes found turned on, even after they had been twice checked.

The bar had once been part of the old Lynch's hotel, but was sold as a separate establishment and the communicating doors to the rest of the building closed off. The paranormal disturbances began almost before the new owner had had a chance to open the doors. Most of the staff could attest to unusual happenings and were reluctant to go up to the storerooms after dark.

While it was true that none of the incidents were harmful, there was a potential for physical injury. Staff had plates and tumblers hurled at them and a crate of cordials were knocked over in a disused passage and the contents hurled down the stairs. One morning the member of staff deputed to open up could not get in the door, as 'someone had stacked crates against it from inside'.

One of the more amusing incidents might lead one to speculate on the gender of the unwelcome guest, because after the bar was closed at night and before the owner or his wife had left the building, they would hear the toilets in the 'Gents' being flushed not once but several times. The owner's wife explained to a reporter, when asked if she had investigated the incidents, that she was 'too much a lady' to go peering about the Gents loo! It did have a social conscience, however, for sometimes 'someone' would carry the cleaner's materials from the Ladies to the Gents to help the early morning cleaner on her way.

Grey Abbey, County Down, was, like Inch, the site for a daughter house to an English community in the twelfth century. In 1193 Affreca, daughter of the King of Man and wife to John De Courcy, founded a community at Grey Abbey, a daughter house to Holme Cultrum Abbey in Cumbria. Located seven miles from Newtownards on the Strangford peninsula, it was a beautiful and well constructed building that would rival her husband's foundation at Inch.

By the time the wars of Edward the Bruce were over (1315–18) the abbey was controlled by the O'Neills of Clandeboye, and when the infamous dissolution of the abbeys took place in 1541, Grey Abbey was but a shadow of its former self. It was burned down in 1573 and only rescued from complete decay when the property was granted to Sir Hugh Montgomery in 1607. Thankfully, at this time the roof was restored and the building established as a parish church. For those visitors interested in architecture, there is a beautiful and elaborate thirteenth century west door, and a fine triple lancet window over the high altar. Included in the buildings were a chapter house and cloister, day-room, parlour and kitchen offices. In all respects it was a typical Cistercian house.

It is self-evident that Grey Abbey exudes a certain tranquillity that can often be found in such locations. There is none of the brooding, sinister atmosphere to be sensed at monastic ruins elsewhere, for example at Quin Abbey, County Clare. As one visitor remarked, a 'holy calm' pervades Grey Abbey. Nor does it have a long or harrowing paranormal history.

There are two incidents, however, worth mentioning. In the early 1960s, a photographer taking pictures in the cloisters suddenly became aware that he was being 'watched'. Turning his head slowly, he saw, standing in the shadow of an archway, a young man clad either in black or dark brown garments. In his arms was what looked like a parcel of books bound with a strap. He was quite well-defined, although the photographer got the impression of a certain wispyness about the edge of the figure. The encounter only lasted a few moments; then the figure walked out of sight. The photographer made a valiant effort to get a shot of the figure, but when the film was developed only the archway appeared clearly. In its centre there was a fuzzy darkness.

The second manifestation was quite unexpected. One evening a friend of the author was waiting for a companion as they strolled about the abbey ruins. He saw on the path to the west door a trio of ladies in full length gowns. As they walked towards him they were chatting together, and the colour of these figures was a misty grey. While the witness was collecting his senses, the figures simply faded away into a mist. His impression of them from a distance was that they were real people. Not having had an experience like this before, he was ill equipped to observe them in detail, but he did get the impression that the costumes worn dated from the early nineteenth century. 'Perhaps they were earlier visitors to the abbey,' he conjectured, 'or a time slip.'

11   Gillhall, County Down

There is a possibility that materials used to build roads, abbeys, castles and the like do have the potential to store information – 'stone tapes', if you like, for stone is a living entity in itself. Some percipients may be more sensitive to this than others and find themselves quite involuntarily 'tuning in' to past events. This may be what caused the elderly lady at Drumbeg to 'see' James Haddock behind the churchyard wall. A very unusual incident was told to me by a medical consultant who had recently holidayed in Athens. He was visiting an amphitheatre there and took time to sit down on one of the stone seats to change his film. 'Suddenly,' he said, 'I found I was not alone but one of many spectators occupying the seats. There seemed to be something going on in the arena. I was so startled that I looked hastily about me, to see how I might make a swift exit. There was a young man sitting one or two feet from me on the same row of seats, and I realized that he was gazing at me with an expression on his face of pure fright! Then, just as swiftly, I was back in the present, with a virtually empty amphitheatre. Did I imagine it? I don't know. And did that long ago spectator see me, as I saw him? It was a very eerie experience, and it only happened after I sat down on the stone seat.'

This was unusual in that it appeared to be a two-way experience. Many experiences are only one way, though nonetheless alarming, and have occurred in castle grounds, stone circles and on roads and bridges.

On the Strangford Road, County Down, there is a small nineteenth century bridge known as 'Fiddler's Bridge'. This bridge may have witnessed a particularly savage killing of a 'man of the road' – a travelling musician, in fact. This man earned a living by travelling from place to place selling his skill with the fiddle, at wakes and weddings and in the local taverns and inns.

It was at such a venue that disaster befell him. One evening, after their day's labour was over, a group of men were drinking their pints in Raholp Inn and the fiddler was playing a tune or two to entertain them. After awhile some of the party called upon the fiddler to play a certain radical 'party tune' with very strong political overtones. The fiddler, conscious that his livelihood depended on all manner of folk, politely declined and struck up a popular reel. Unfortunately his audience, now 'fighting drunk', waylaid the fiddler later along the road and beat him to death. Once they had committed this fearful deed, and well aware what retribution would follow in its wake, they set about hiding the body.

They took hold of their victim and carried him along a narrow track, known as 'the Scraw Pad', which wound around the village and came out on a stretch of road that the men themselves were constructing between Downpatrick and Strangford. There they dug a shallow grave and laid the fiddler in it.

Some days later, after heavy rain, the murderers found to their consternation that the corpse was partially exposed, so with one or two keeping watch they re-buried the fiddler. As there is no record of the murder having been discovered or the miscreants being arrested, we have to conclude that they got away with the horrid deed. Certainly the grave, said to be near the bridge, was never found and it was only many years later that a deathbed confession from one of the killers revealed the fiddler's fate.

Within sight of the bridge, local tradition has it that flickering lights are seen, shining like lanterns, and horses take fright on the bridge itself. Perhaps this is yet another case of the fabric of the bridge retaining some imprint of that night.

The lovely Kingdom of Mourne in County Down has a wealth of folklore and legend to attract the student in such matters and, as with many an account, there are 'grains of truth' in some of these tales. One persistent tale in the vicinity of Hillton, in Mourne country, is that of 'the Phantom Sower'. This apparition was seen regularly over a period of about thirty years in the early part of this century. In the early evening the apparition would appear from a site of ancient stones, called the Druid's Circle, on top of Goward Hill. It would be wrapped in a large white 'Sower's apron' and would go through the motions of scattering seed onto the ground. This nightly ritual was witnessed by many, and the actions of the apparition never varied. Then, quite inexplicably, the phantom vanished not to be seen again. A local man who was something of a practical joker decided to 'revive' the phantom sower after some time had elapsed. Dressed in a sheet and suitable make-up, he set forth for the Druid's Circle after broadcasting the news that 'the Sower' had manifested again.

Obviously the real phantom was not amused, for hardly had the fraudulent 'Sower' commenced his act then the real ghost took up his stance behind him. The practical joker came to the uneasy conclusion that he was being followed and, whirling about, to his horror was confronted by the apparition. With a yell of pure fright the joker tore off his sheet and fled as though the very Devil were after him.

The following year, at the time of the spring sowing, a farmer and his labourer were indulging in some land reclamation near the Druid's Circle when they came across the skeleton of a man wrapped in a rotting 'Sowing sheet'. The skull showed signs of having been badly battered. A coroner's investigation subsequently brought to light a gruesome tale of two men hired for the sowing of crops years before. A terrible quarrel had broken out between the two, and one had felled the other with his spade. Then, realizing what he had done, the murderer fled. There had been at the time little curiosity about the two itinerants, and in the end their sudden disappearance had been forgotten – until the discovery of the remains lapped in a rotting sower's sheet that had become the unfortunate man's shroud.

Another phantom seen in the Hillsborough district of County Down was of much more recent stock. In the winter of 1985 a middle-aged couple were driving down the Hillsborough Road towards their home in County Tyrone. Visibility was good, and there was no other traffic on the road.

Suddenly they saw on their side of the road a young girl kneeling or squatting on the roadway. The wife was overcome by a strong feeling of apprehension and begged her husband to drive on, an entirely alien action for so kindly a couple. They both had a strange reluctance to discuss the episode, but eventually they did. By now they had their suspicions that it might be linked to a tragedy that had occurred on the

Belfast/Dublin motorway when a young woman had been killed in a collision between her car and one travelling on the wrong side of the motorway. Very soon after the accident, there was a spate of reports of a young woman answering her description being seen standing on the hard shoulder. Sometimes motorists actually claimed to have picked her up, only for the girl to vanish after a few hundred yards. The manifestation did not always take place in the same spot but could change from one side of the road to the other.

Physical descriptions given by witnesses largely matched one another with regard to what she was wearing – it was claimed that she had on a tweed coat, carried neither handbag nor gloves and was hatless. This was almost exactly what the couple on the Hillsborough road described also. When they looked back, she was gone.

This kind of report of what has become known as 'the phantom hitchhiker' is common to most parts of Western Europe and North America. Sometimes there appear to be links to fatal accidents that have happened on that stretch of the road. Sometimes the apparition simply stands beside the road; sometimes it seems to indicate that it wants a lift. A common factor is the three-dimensional 'normal' appearance of the figure that has caused motorists to stop and offer assistance. The traumatic effect of a passenger who suddenly vanishes from the car after a few yards can be imagined.

Another road phantom in County Down was reported by Mr D., a bank manager, who was driving from his home in Hillsborough, County Down, to Newry, a border town. It happened about 8.30 a.m. one fine June morning on the old road from Hillsborough and about three miles from Banbridge, County Down.

As he drove along, Mr D. saw beside the road, a few yards from a gate into a field, a young soldier in uniform, apparently waiting for a lift. He was not hitchhiking but appeared to be expecting someone. Mr D. explained:

The soldier was wearing a khaki great coat and a forage cap. He had a kitbag slung over his shoulder and gaiters or puttees on his boots. The reason I can be so specific is that I had slowed down in case of an army checkpoint, and so I had time to notice these things. As I passed him, he gave no sign of noticing me, and he carried no weapon. He was quite substantial in appearance, if a little pale. I was a good hundred yards past him when the full impact of what I had seen hit me. I looked in the rearview mirror, but the road was empty ...

Mr D. reversed back along the road to the gate. Then he got out and looked up and down the road and into the field, but there was no one to be seen. He was quite emphatic that no vehicle had passed him in either direction that might have picked up the soldier. He agreed with the suggestion that the soldier might have gone into the field, but why should he hide? He had shown no alarm when Mr D. had seen him the first time.

Mr D.'s puzzlement is understandable. Over the last quarter of a century the residents of Northern Ireland have become all too familiar with the sight of Army personnel on their roads. But members of H.M. Forces seldom stroll about the countryside on their own. They are always in fully-manned patrols and wear combat kit. This soldier, on a hot June day, was wearing a heavy army coat and forage cap and was not armed. Mr D. explained that the style of dress was very 'dated' and not what he, as an ex-soldier himself, would have expected to see. He repeated that the soldier was 'real' and appeared to be waiting in a purposeful fashion. The whole event lasted about twenty to thirty seconds, from the time when he first saw the figure to the time he stopped the car and reversed back. The interesting point is that had the soldier been dressed conventionally, Mr D. would not have given him a second glance and probably would have assumed that the rest of the patrol were in the field. It was something 'odd' about him that had caught Mr D.'s attention.

Subsequent enquiry showed that there had been no military incident on that stretch of road, and the conclusion arrived at was that Mr D. had encountered a soldier of World War Two, or possibly World War One. The wearing of puttees may have led to this conclusion. The apparition, as far as is ascertainable, was not seen by anyone else, either before Mr D. or after. One wonders if the witness, with his mind in a state of rest, had 'picked up' the image of a soldier who at some past time had waited quite legitimately at that spot for a lift into town.

Mercifully, paranormal events associated with the 'Troubles' of the last twenty-five years in Northern Ireland have been few and far between. Only two incidents come to mind as being well attested to. One was the apparition of a soldier that manifested from time to time beside the lift shaft of a block of flats in West Belfast, a figure seen by a number of residents. A soldier had in fact been murdered in the area. The second incident, on a much wider scale, had connections with an appalling ambush that took place near Rostrevor in County Down. On an autumn evening in 1980, a local man was driving home along the road between Warrenpoint and Newry. It was about 9 p.m. and already dark. The road runs along the side of Carlingford Lough, which at this point is a natural boundary with the Republic of Ireland.

The witness was alone in the car and listening to the radio as he approached Narrow Water Castle, an ancient square battlement tower beside the road. It had been built by the McGennis chiefs in about 1560. Then, ahead of him, the motorist saw a powerful light being swung in an arc from the roadside – a familiar 'Stop' signal for an army or police checkpoint. He slowed down for what he took to be a road block, and as he drew to a halt he could see beneath the trees a number of soldiers carrying rifles and one soldier in combat gear wielding the torch.

The witness came to a stop, switched off his headlights and wound down his window as he waited to be approached. A soldier came to the window, asked for his driving licence and requested him to open the car boot. The witness got out of the car and moved to the back of the car, expecting the soldier to follow. Then the witness said that he began to feel most peculiar, and 'a great cold shiver ran over him'. He became aware that 'something was horribly wrong'. As he stood there, he realized the soldier was nowhere to be seen and his driving licence was lying on the ground at the driver's door. Now very frightened indeed, the witness ran to the front of the car and peered into the dark. There were no patrol vehicles, no troops, in fact no sign of anyone on the road save himself. The patrol simply wasn't there.

Between June, 1980 and March, 1981 there were two other similar incidents at the same spot. In each case the witnesses alleged that they had been flagged down and that a single soldier had approached their cars. They, too, had seen other figures moving about. In each case the patrol suddenly vanished, leaving some very terrified people behind on the empty road. Only the first witness, however, alleged that the soldier spoke to him. Upon each occasion the details were reported to others, including a parish priest, and there was no way the witnesses could be persuaded to alter their accounts.

It is important to recall that in August, 1979 eighteen British soldiers were lured into an ambush by the IRA at this spot and brutally murdered. Even in the long catalogue of Ulster's troubles this incident stands out both for its scale and the unforgettable barbarity of the deed.

What paranormalists have had to ask is whether the witnesses 'picked up' vibrations of that dreadful slaughter, or did they find themselves in some kind of 'time slip' which involved a road block and a military patrol? We have no way of identifying the soldier that approached the car as being one of the soldiers murdered in the ambush. It is not unusual for motorists to suffer hallucinations or some form of ESP when driving in a state of relaxation over familiar territory, their minds being set on 'automatic pilot' as it were.

With three incidents at the same spot, witnessed on one occasion by a group of three people, one has to ask if what they experienced might have had some connection with the Narrow Water Castle ambush. After the incidents, a group of local people led by members of the clergy said prayers at the spot, and in recent years there have been no further reports.

Dromore, County Down, is a quiet market town with many ecclesiastical connections. St Colman is said to have built an abbey here, and the town became the seat of a long line of bishops, the most noted being Jeremy Taylor (1661–7) and Thomas Percy (1782–1811). Their remains lie within the cathedral. To the northeast lies a greate motte and bailey, about 200 feet in diameter, and on the outskirts lies the Gillhall estate.

The great house, once the heart of the estate, is there no more. It was destroyed in a fire in the 1970s, and there are no remains to mark the spot where once stood a dwelling central to one of the strangest hauntings ever recorded. There was more than one paranormal manifestation at Gillhall, although some of the most important incidents were separated by more than two centuries. The manifestations appeared to have little or no connection to one another, save that they happened in the same house and surrounding area.

The tale of the Beresford Ghost is well known in the annals of Irish hauntings and indeed is known outside of Ireland through writers such as Le Fanu. I would like to record my thanks to the Clanwilliam family and, in particular, the late Lord Clanwilliam, who was kind enough to give me access to family papers which gave clear and unambiguous accounts of the alleged manifestation.

The story of Gillhall begins with the account of the friendship of James De La Poer, Third Earl of Tyrone, and Nicola Sophia Hamilton, daughter of Baron Hugh Hamilton of Glenawley. It seems that both these young people were orphaned at an early age and were to be placed under the care of the same person who, as the papers say, 'educated them in the principles of Deism' – that is to say, a belief in the existence of a God but not in any revealed religion in particular.

When they were about fourteen years of age they were removed to the care of another tutor, who endeavoured to eradicate their former philosophy but only managed to create a great deal of confusion in their adolescent minds. Out of this confusion arose the well-known promise that each gave to the other: namely, that whoever died first would return from the dead to tell the survivor which religion was favoured by the Supreme Deity.

In the fullness of time Nicola married Sir Tristram Beresford M.P. and Tyrone married a Miss Rickards. They continued to be friends and the four young people spent a great deal of time in one another's company. In October, 1693 Sir Tristram and Lady Beresford were on a visit to Nicola's sister at Gillhall. Nicola was expecting her third child. She already had two small daughters and now hoped for an heir.

She awoke in the early hours of the morning at Gillhall to find the apparition of Lord Tyrone standing beside her bed while her husband slept deeply beside her. The apparition told her that he had died the previous Tuesday at four o'clock, unknown to her, and that in fulfilment of their old promise he had come to reveal to her what religion was favoured by the Almighty. The conversation that ensued implied that the Almighty favoured the pursuit of a revealed religion, while not going into denominational details, and that only by supporting Mother Church might a sinner be saved.

Lord Tyrone also told Nicola that she would have a son and heir, and that the child would eventually grow up to marry his own heiress. He told her too that her husband would only live a short while after the birth of the heir and that she herself would wed a second time 'to a man whose ill treatment will render you miserable', and that she would die in her forty-seventh year in childbirth. Showing great strength of mind, Nicola Beresford asked Tyrone to leave some tangible proof of his visitation. He responded by looping the heavy bed curtains in such a fashion that Nicola could not have done the deed on her own, and he inscribed his name in her pocket-book that lay on the night table. Still Nicola was not satisfied. 'I could have performed these deeds in my sleep,' she said. Then Lord Tyrone took hold of her wrist with fingers as burning as fire, yet as cold as death. With more than one lingering look, he faded away.

Next morning Nicola replaced the bed curtains with the help of a broom and locked the pocket-book in her desk; her wrist she bound up in a black riband, saying to her husband, 'Let me conjure you, Sir Tristram, never to enquire the cause of me wearing this ribbon; for you will never again see me without it. If it concerned you as a husband, I would not for a moment conceal it; I never in my life refused your request, but for this ...'

Whether Sir Tristram assumed that, as his wife was in a 'delicate condition', she must at all costs be humoured, we do not know. But he honoured his word and never again referred to the riband. Later that day came news by messenger of Lord Tyrone's death at the time that the phantom had told Nicola, and the other prophecies were to come true as well. Nicola did give birth to a son, and Sir Tristram did die when that child was only eight.

The young widow became something of a recluse, understandably, bearing in mind the dire prophecy about a second marriage. Her excursions were rare, mostly confined to visiting a clergyman and his wife in the village where she resided. The clergyman had a son, a young officer some years Nicola's junior, and despite the ghostly warning she fell in love and married the Lieutenant General Gorges. The sad prophecy came true, for when the novelty of being married to a lovely heiress wore off, Gorges treated Nicola quite abominably until, in despair, she left him.

Some time later, however, after signs of penitence from the young man and to please her in-laws, Nicola consented to live with him again and was soon pregnant for the fourth time. She expected to go into labour on or about her birthday, and accordingly she sent for a few friends to have a little celebration. She believed herself to be forty-eight, and was heartily thankful that the prophecy about dying in her forty-seventh year at least had proved erroneous. Alas, the elderly clergyman who had christened her told her that there had been a family confusion about her age. He had consulted the register and found that in fact she was only forty-seven.

At this Nicola grew pale and told her friends to leave her for 'her death warrant had been signed' and she retired to her chamber, along with her friend Lady Massereene and her son Marcus, now a lad of fourteen. She then revealed all that had taken place those many years before and instructed Marcus to unbind her wrist once she was dead. A short time later she went into protracted labour and died in great agony. When Marcus unbound her wrist he found it scarred and shrivelled, or as the manuscripts say, 'every nerve withered, every sinew shrunk'.

I am indebted to Sir Shane Leslie who in his *Ghost Book* confirms that the apparition visited Nicola at Gillhall, and that he had seen the original ribbon preserved by a member of the family. The portrait of Nicola wearing the ribbon does not appear to have survived. It must be pointed out that the visitation was a once-only affair: only Nicola, Lady Beresford, was witness to it. For those interested, the rest of Lord Tyrone's prophecy came true as well, for Marcus did marry Catherine, Lord Tyrone's heiress, and their children were famous in their own right: One became Archbishop of Tuam; another, the Hon. John Beresford, earned the title 'king of Ireland' on account of his powerful influence in Irish affairs; and the third became the First Marquis of Waterford.

In effect, one cannot say that Gillhall was haunted by the ghost of Lord Tyrone, for in fact wherever Nicola had been that night she would have received his visitation. There was more to come, however, as far as Gillhall was concerned, and in the 1960s it achieved a certain notoriety. There had been isolated tales of disturbances over the centuries, but no more than might be connected to any great and historic house. For instance, in the nineteenth century any guest put to sleep in the room directly beside the 'porte cochère' might hear in the night the rumbling of a coach, and on rising would see a young woman descend from the coach and run up the steps. This manifestation was seen long after the porte cochère was removed.

Lord Clanwilliam and his family had lived in Gillhall before removing to the family seat at Montalto, County Down. During the moving a strange incident took place. The family possessed a valuable but 'cursed' mirror that had been handed down from generation to generation. It was said that if a member of the family looked in the mirror, they would surely die. So to counter an 'accident', the mirror was hung so far up a wall that there was no possibility of a stray glance! During removal, the mirror was taken down and carefully crated for its installation at Montalto. It lay there overnight, and in the morning when Lord Clanwilliam came to fetch it the crate gave off an ominous tinkling sound. The crate was opened only for them to find that the mirror lay in a thousand pieces, 'none larger than my finger nail,' said Lord Clanwilliam ruefully. How this could have occurred was a complete mystery, as no one had been in the house that night and the crate lay just as it had been left.

In June, 1961, while the house was unoccupied, a local amateur tape recording society got permission to record in the house overnight. What was recorded on those tapes was sufficiently mystifying for the society members to seek further clarification. While hesitant about applying the label 'haunted', nevertheless the thumps, bangs, and sounds of footsteps in the house gave pause for thought. One or two members of the Clanwilliam family had mentioned apparitions in the house, one of a 'fat, repulsive man in a nightshirt' on the staircase, and another of 'a goose' that walked the lower corridor and which metamorphosised into a shapeless white mass.

There was a traditional 'haunted room' in the house, where a young woman had burned to death in the seventeenth century, but in the 1960s this was an area not really affected by manifestations that emanated mostly from the cellar and cellar stairs, the main staircase and one or two of the empty rooms on the ground and first floor. There were a number of investigations, which included wiring the house for sound and relaying the information onto a bank of speakers and recording equipment. While every conceivable kind of noise could be heard through the speakers, ranging from voices to the sound of flames crackling and furniture being dragged about in rooms where there was no furniture, when one attempted to listen without electronic aid the house would settle into an eerie silence. Other physical manifestations included doors that opened of their own accord or locked themselves with no assistance and heavy pieces of iron piping being flung about the cellar. One could also hear the sound of fingernails being drawn down a microphone, fifteen foot up a wall.

Most unnerving of all was that in a kennel run at the back of the house, the gamekeeper to the estate kept a number of gun dogs which forty or fifty seconds before a manifestation inside the house would howl in ever increasing volume. The temperature in the house was freezing, despite a mild June night, and one had the distinct sensation of being 'watched'.

While the activity at Gillhall was at its height a number of groups, including members of the Churches Fellowship for Psychical Study, visited the house and experienced what can only be termed its 'Jekyll and Hyde' character: during the hours of darkness all manner of manifestation took place, while from dawn until dusk it was simply an old and gracious house.

Over the years following the tragic fire that was to destroy Gillhall, there have been isolated incidents of paranormal activity. Within the last decade a taxi driver, taking home a late fare on the main road past the front gates of the estate, saw a coach and four on the road ahead, which then turned at right angles and passed right through a portion of the demesne wall. On another occasion a local girl waiting at a request stop on the same road saw a woman dressed in Victorian garb coming down the front avenue, as though heading for the bus. According to the witness the woman did not board the bus, nor could she be seen anywhere on the road.

Gillhall also has had a peculiar contempt for modern media techniques. Television crews experienced great difficulty in getting cameras and sound equipment to work once they were in close proximity to the house. Members of those crews were quite likely to be bombarded with slates which would fall from the roof even on the calmest day. One woman journalist, unable to get into the house, applied her eye to the letterbox on the main door and was rewarded with a view of the very graceful oak staircase leading from the hall to the first floor. Several days later she returned to the house with a photographer. Once inside she discovered that it was impossible to see the stairs via the front door letterbox, as the back of the door was shielded by a large piece of steel plate, completely obscuring the letterbox slit. 'Yet, I did see the stairs quite clearly! I know I did,' she told her companion.

Another pair of Sunday newspaper journalists from England had a more unpleasant encounter. They had been referred to the author for information, and it seemed incumbent on their informant that she should warn them of the 'pitfalls' of attempting to photograph the house. It was obvious that they had a somewhat romantic attitude towards 'the quaintness' of the Irish, and they assured the author that they would be perfectly alright. They would, however, put her mind at ease by calling in to see her on the way back to their hotel, after they had taken their pictures.

An hour or so later two wet and rather sober journalists stood again on the doorstep. Their tale was one of considerable woe. They had found Gillhall easily. Then, halfway up the long back drive, the car stalled and flatly refused to start up again. The two young men were forced to take their equipment and cover the remaining quarter of a mile or so on foot. Only yards from the car the heavens opened and they were deluged with very heavy rain. Not to be beaten, they struggled on until one of the men received a blow between the shoulder blades that precipitated him into a ditch. Although his companion vigorously protested that he was innocent of any misdeed, there was no one else around to blame. Finally, when they came to check their equipment, they found that an essential battery was flat, even though the equipment had only recently been thoroughly checked. By now, wholly dispirited and not a little apprehensive, they returned to the car. To their astonishment, with one turn of the ignition the car burst into life, and as they made their way out of the gates they couldn't help but notice that the road outside the gates was bone dry!

On a more serious note, it has to be said that in terms of paranormal disturbances Gillhall has been among the most prolific in the annals of Irish hauntings. But there was something else. Paranormal happenings, from a research point of view, are regarded not as acts of a supernatural cause but wholly within the natural law. The fact that we do not understand that law does not negate its effects. Yet at Gillhall one had an underlying sense of menace. In good old fashioned terms, one would have spoken of a 'sense of evil' that seemed to hold sway in the place. As one seasoned researcher remarked after a particularly noisy night in the house, 'There was a point where I was afraid for my immortal soul!' An extravagant statement? Perhaps, but there were other sensible, scientifically-oriented folk who felt exactly the same. It may be that there are 'more things in heaven and earth than are dreamt of in our philosophy'.

12 The Little Lad of Tempo

County Fermanagh is one of the best known of Northern counties to visitors from all over the world. The long course of the River Erne flowing through the county, with the well known Upper and Lower Lough Erne, is the haunt of anglers, naturalists and boat enthusiasts. The Loughs are particularly notable for their many richly wooded islands, some containing remains of ancient churches and prehistoric sites. There are several cave systems in the area too, the best known being Marble Arch. Historic houses also recall the past, and some are now in the care of the National Trust, such as the beautiful Castlecoole, Florencecourt and the seat of the Earl of Erne, Crom Castle, which is the site of one particular mystery, the 'White Light of Crom'. This manifestation appears over Lough Erne as a rolling ball of white light and precedes events of great moment, either to the country as a whole or to the Erne family in particular. There are the ruins too of 'Plantation Castles' which bear witness to the stormy history of Fermanagh, and the fine historic town of Enniskillen with its long military associations.

Tempo Manor in the village of Tempo, not far from Enniskillen, has a tale that is both piteable and gruesome. In the sixteenth century the manor was in the possession of the Maguire chief, who by all accounts was both brutal and dishonest. During his incumbency horse races were run at Tempo and, for those travelling long distances to attend, masters, grooms and horses were put up by the Maguires. In the course of two or three days, a great deal of money would change hands both by fair means and foul, as a good deal of 'persuasion' could be meted out to stable lads to ensure that their charges ran in a fashion that lined the pockets of those with the greatest financial interest.

The lad of whom this story is told was by all accounts both

good and honest. It has been surmised that he met his brutal end because he refused to be party to some underhanded gambling. An angry owner, possibly the Maguire himself, murdered the boy and hid the body under a flagstone in the stable block. The story passed into legend, and for many years little or no attempt was made to prove it right or wrong. Then, some three hundred years later, in the earlier part of this century, one of the Langham family, now in possession of the manor, decided to investigate.

The flagstone at the stable door was dug up, and underneath it was discovered a pathetic bundle of rags and remains – all that was left of the stable lad, it was surmised. The skull of the child was brought into the house for closer examination and housed in a small museum belonging to the master of the house, who cherished an interest in natural history. It was said that the child's skull was put with a collection of monkey skulls already in the museum.

From the moment that the skull was brought indoors, the household experienced a number of disturbances. The family dog even refused to go up the stairs to the museum corridor. Several members of the household suffered small but painful accidents, and much unease was occasioned by these events. Finally the owner decided that enough was enough and the skull, together with the rest of the remains, was buried secretly in the shrubbery in a spot that was known only to the family. Almost at once the disturbances in the house ceased.

But out in the stable yard matters were still problematical, especially in the vicinity of the loosebox at whose door the remains had been found. The Langhams found difficulty in housing livestock in the loosebox. On one occasion, when a small group of pedigree calves were housed there, they worked themselves into such a panic that one jumped through a window and injured itself very badly. Horses stabled in the box overnight would be found in the morning soaked in sweat and on the verge of hysteria. After a number of such incidents, the loosebox was turned into a store and the disturbances ceased. Having personally viewed the plain grey flag and the box in question, I came away with a sense of gloom and a feeling of horrified pity for the little lad who had been faithful to his charge and who had paid for his loyalty with his life. For him life had been 'nasty, brutish and short'.

* * *

Another animal which figures in Fermanagh's history of the paranormal is a greyhound who, in the 1940s, belonged to schoolteacher Kevin McNally. Kevin and his family had always had greyhounds about the place, and one evening he heard a great scratching and whining at the door of his father's farmhouse near Lisnaskea, County Fermanagh. When the door was opened they found one of the greyhounds in a great state of shock. It was obvious that the animal had had some kind of traumatic experience, although there were no signs of physical injury.

When Kevin's elderly father arrived home some minutes later, he too was in an agitated state of mind. The reason became clear as the story unfolded. He and the dog had been taking an evening stroll across the fields towards a derelict cottage that had for some years stood on family land. As they headed for a gap in the hedge, the father could see clearly across to the cottage, and he saw approaching the selfsame gap an elderly lady dressed all in black. As it was obvious that they would confront one another at the hedge, Kevin's father stood back to let her through, bidding her 'Good night' as he did so. To his consternation, within quite literally feet of him, the old lady vanished and, at the same moment, the greyhound – normally a friendly and placid animal – gave a yelp and, tearing the leash from his owner's hand, fled hell-for-leather across the field.

Kevin then took up the story, confirming the dog's condition when he arrived at the door. 'When I let him in, he was in a terrible state, trembling and whining. He could not be persuaded to leave the house for over a day.' All Kevin's father could say was that he did not recognize the woman and she had not uttered a word. 'Nor,' he added, 'could she have gone out of my sight, for the gap was in the middle of the field which one could view quite plainly for a substantial distance. I could not see her anywhere.' Further enquiry revealed nothing about the previous owner of the cottage, which had lain in ruins from the end of the nineteenth century.

There are, as has been said, a number of Plantation Castle ruins around the shores of Lough Erne. Among these, on the south shore, is Tully Castle, built by Sir John Hume in about 1610 and destroyed by Rory Maguire in 1641. Southwest of the castle lie the loughs of Carrick and Bannahone, which hold between them the lovely Correl Glen with its gracious wooded slopes. The castle was a fine, sturdy example of all that was best in Plantation Castles, with its grey/fawn stone Bawn and its good defensive structure. The remains of its wall and foundations imply a home and battlement of some significance. Alas, these attributes were not to save its defenders on Christmas Day, 1641, when virtually all the inhabitants of Tully were murdered by Rory Maguire.

While not a site with a great history of haunting, in the early 1960s two almost identical events were noted by visitors to the site in broad daylight. The weather was fine and the visibility good. In both instances the witnesses were on the shoreward side of Tully. Neither man knew the other, and neither was familiar with the history of the castle.

The first witness had sat down on a stone to tie his shoelace when he looked up and saw, less than one hundred yards away, two figures leading their horses at a fast trot across the outer foundations of the castle. One man carried a staff or a pike. His face was quite distinct and he appeared to have a chest wound. The witness only saw him briefly, then he faded away into the background. The other figure appeared to lose hold of his horse, and he fell to the ground and vanished as well. The witness's impression of him was of a 'tall, swarthy man'. He admitted to having been very frightened and his impressions 'hazy'.

The second witness, who had just come into the area, could see the first witness seated on the stone but noticed nothing else at first. Then he too saw the apparitions, the horses and 'a pike'. But in his case the apparitions went out of sight behind a wall and did not reappear. He described the figures as 'faint and grey'. The two men compared notes and concluded that the figures were wearing some kind of body armour. Although the armour was not very clearly seen, the pike or staff was. One witness, who was staying locally, mentioned the incident to his hosts, who told him that while there was no firm tradition of Tully Castle being haunted, there had been local reports of lights and figures being seen there, especially at Christmas time.

The latterday visitor to Castle Archdale will remember it better as a leisure centre and marina than an historic site. The Archdale family, who came from Norfolk, built two fine castles on a thousand-acre site beside the Erne. It was purchased in 1610 for the princely sum of £506.08. The square towers of Castle Archdale are long laid waste, but on Castle Hill, a date plate with the inscription '1610' may still be seen. As far as is known the second castle, built on the foundations of the first, had no strong paranormal associations or 'resident ghost'.

The 1775 additions to the older part of the castle have now vanished as well, with the exception of a sympathetically restored courtyard and stable area. There is, however, a later haunting recalled in modern times which took place in the upstairs apartments of the stable block staff quarters, situated over the old kitchens and adjacent to the corridor connecting the kitchen block to the main house.

Mr Ian Braund, the warden of the Castle Archdale Centre, explained. In 1976/7 he and his young family were occupying the kitchen quarters, consisting of three bedrooms and lower floor dayrooms. While he occupied the main bedroom, his children occupied two rooms divided from their father's by a corridor which ran along the stone retaining wall of the old quarters. The children's room had originally been a dormitory for the female staff, but the rooms had been partitioned by wood taken from the old wardrobes in the dormitory. The little girl slept in the front room and the child continually complained of the cold. Even her father admitted to the room being 'eerie'. He did not, of course, say this to his daughter, but even in daylight she was reluctant to use the room.

Then his daughter began to have nightmares and fits of screaming. She told her father that late at night a man and a dog would enter the room and the dog would jump up and lick her face. She said that the man 'encouraged' the dog to do this, and that the man wore 'funny clothes'. Finally the child became so distressed she was moved into her brother's room. All talk of man and dog ceased, and the small boy, when asked, said he had never seen the man and dog.

Some time later Mr Braund was speaking to his employer, Mr Denis Archdale, and discovered that almost ten years before his daughter's experiences Mr Archdale's children, who had been put to bed in the selfsame room, had also seen the apparitional man and dog. The Archdale children had been quite upset and described how the man was dressed in old fashioned clothes, while the dog was described as 'being like Goldie', their own

Golden Labrador, but black in colour.

If the children were not suffering from joint hallucinations, then one has to consider other possibilities. The haunted room was panelled in wood taken from the old house, and the flight of stairs was also from the old house and had been re-used in the stable block. Ian Braund noted that quite often when he passed the haunted room the door would be open and he would close it, but if he walked back past the door again it would be open once more. Did the use of these materials have anything to do with the children's vision of a man and dog? Piecing together the sketchy description, two possibilities exist for the presence of the man. One is that the description of the clothes could suggest a gamekeeper. However, the men on staff had never slept in this part of the yard, although they would have used it daily. The breeches and gaiters described by the children could suggest the working clothes of the nineteenth century or even earlier. Of course the figure could have been 'imported' with the panelling, and the apparition may have represented a member of the earlier family.

When an elderly woman who had served at the 'big house' in the capacity of a dairymaid was consulted, she confirmed that the family had dogs and that the estate keepers would have been up and down the yard several times a day. But she had never heard of a haunting in her day, which would have been early this century. There had been no tragedy or crime to her knowledge. In fact among the great houses in the area Castle Archdale had been singularly free of paranormal events. The only tales she knew concerned the bansidhe that walked by the lake, and another of a 'little old woman' who could be encountered in the woods. Locals said she too was a 'fairy woman' and fearfully ugly!

There is, however, a curse on Castle Archdale which has to do with the castle of 1773. When the house was being built, stones were taken from Kiltierney Abbey, some few miles away. This action was, as in the case of the Finnebrogue Gates, considered most inadvisable, for they were consecrated stones. A curse therefore followed the despoilers. It was believed that no Archdale heir would ever be born alive in the castle, so when her time came for 'lying in' the lady of Archdale always went elsewhere to bear her offspring.

* * *

Poltergeist activity has already been alluded to in these pages, and it is undoubtedly true that some of the best documented cases of this kind of manifestation have occurred in Ireland. The poltergeist of Derrygonelly, County Fermanagh, attracted a great deal of attention, including the participation of Sir William Barrett, President of the London Society for Psychical Research. The manifestation took place in the last century, in a small farmhouse about eleven miles from Enniskillen. The afflicted family consisted of a farmer and his family of four girls and a boy, of whom the eldest, Maggie, was a girl of about twenty. The cottage was a typical one consisting of three rooms – a kitchen and two rooms leading off that served as bedrooms. Maggie slept in one with her sisters and it was in this room that the majority of the disturbances occurred. They consisted of knocks and scratchings. Also, items of clothing and boots were flung about, and there was difficulty in keeping even a single candle lit in the house.

The farmer himself was a non-conformist, and once it was clear that 'rats' were not the cause he had sought help from his church elders. They had suggested placing the Holy Book in the room and, as a precaution, the farmer had put a heavy stone on it to keep it in place. However, some unseen agency removed the stone and in a fit of pique tore seventeen pages out of the Bible.

Among the more alarming manifestations were showers of pebbles that hurtled through the air and frightened the children in their beds. As well as this, the children were pinched and slapped by some unseen hand.

At this point, Sir William Barrett was invited to come and see for himself. The eminent investigator had a blow by blow account from the farmer and later he described his own observations: 'After the children, except the boy, had gone to bed, Maggie lay down on the bed without undressing, so that her hands and feet could be observed ... faint raps increasing in loudness were heard coming apparently from the walls, the ceilings and other areas of the inner room, the door of which was open ... the closest scrutiny failed to detect any movement on the part of those present. Suddenly a large pebble fell in my presence on the bed ...' Sir William likened the knocks to a carpenter's hammer driving nails into flooring.

After having satisfied himself that no one present was playing a trick, Sir William invited another member of the SPR to join him. This was the theological scholar the Rev. Maxwell Close. Together with a Mr Plunkett from Enniskillen, the three men spent two more nights at the cottage. The house and surrounding grounds were searched repeatedly, but nothing was found. Finally the group of experts gave up and prepared to leave, whereupon the farmer, overcome with anxiety, told Sir William that they had tested 'it' by asking it questions, and that 'it' told lies as well as truth. Sir William tested the entity by asking for raps to coincide with numbers he thought of, and this time four answers were correct. But still they were no nearer finding out the mystery. Finally, the Rev. Maxwell Close read some passages of Scripture and asked the assembled company to join him in the Lord's Prayer. At first the noises were so loud the words of the prayer could scarcely be heard, but gradually all became quiet and from that time on there was no further disturbance. Later, when the farmer was asked for his opinion, he said he thought it was 'the fairies'. Similar events have happened in areas as wide apart as Antrim and Tipperary where showers of stones, potatoes and turf have been hurled, and often the presence of several kinds of clergy had no appreciable effect at all.

Sir William's own theory of a 'radiant centre' presupposed that someone was the focus of whatever energy created the disturbances; in this case, he thought Maggie was the centre because, when she was absent, the disturbances were sometimes appreciably less. Certainly, over the years, the pattern of poltergeist disturbances has changed very little, save in the adaptation to modern day life. Now the disturbances may focus on electric bulbs instead of candles and on telephone bells instead of knockings on the door.

13   Springhill, County Londonderry

County Londonderry takes its name from a charter given to some of the London Companies by James the First. It extends from the shores of Lough Foyle along an Atlantic seaboard to Lough Neagh in the southwest. Locally, the county tends to be called 'Derry' from 'Doire', an oak grove. It consists mainly of hills, with the Sperrin Mountains on the County Tyrone border to the southeast and the heights of Slieve Gullion to the west. The city of Londonderry is a fine historical one, with its famous walls and the echoes of the notorious siege of 1689.

In the early 1980s a Miss F.H. of Londonderry set out with her brother one evening to visit a very sick friend in a nursing home in the city. It was a dank and chill winter's evening and the pair stepped out briskly along the city street. When they came to the end of their road and were preparing to cross to the other side, in the direction of the nursing home, they saw a black horse-drawn hearse, with the horses decked in plumes and black ribbons, coming up the road beside them. As it passed by they noticed that the hearse was empty, and there was no following cortege. It struck Miss F.H. that it was rather curious that at such a late hour (nearly twilight) the hearse was not going towards the cemetery or indeed to the livery stables close by but heading toward the city.

The conveyance made no noise, nor could the brother and sister recall seeing a driver, and they were both seized by a strange unease. They made little comment, however, but quickened their steps towards the nursing home. When they arrived there they were told that their friend had taken a sudden turn for the worse and had died shortly before their arrival. 'Just about the time we saw the black hearse travelling in this direction,' remarked Miss F.H.

The fact that they had seen a hearse of some antiquity was not in itself unusual, for up until the 1950s and 1960s this kind of vehicle was still used by some funeral directors for special funerals. So this in itself would not have excited much curiosity. What had struck the couple more strongly was the silence of its passage, the lateness of the hour and the presumption that the hearse was going to fetch its occupant rather than returning from a funeral. 'There was no noise of horses or the jangle of their bits, and I simply cannot recall a driver,' reiterated Miss F.H., 'no matter how odd that sounds.'

While it is true that the 'black coach' is not a purely Irish phenomenon but has been reported in both English and Scottish traditions, it is also possible that in the nineteenth century, when body snatching was both a macabre and a lucrative trade, the tradition of a 'black coach' traversing the roads at night and arousing quite irrational fears in some folk may have been cultivated as a distinct advantage to those who engaged in this evil practice. Thus, the apprehension aroused in both Miss F.H. and her brother may have been connected subliminally with this unhappy tradition.

Black is, of course, a colour that carries with it a sense of doom, and 'the black dog' or 'the black coach' might not have been viewed with such trepidation had they sported some other colour. In 1928 a university student was fishing in one of Derry's waterways when he saw coming towards him along the deserted river bank a large black dog. It was of such a ferocious size that the young man abandoned his fishing gear with some speed and climbed into a tree. As the dog passed beneath the branch, it lifted its head and snarled at the young fisherman. Happily, the dog seemed to have pressing business elsewhere and passed on by, but the dog's eyes were recalled fearfully by the young angler. 'They were huge and red, and they blazed as though a fire was lit behind them.' This particular 'black dog' was well known to have its beat along the river bank and the young man's tale was readily believed.

Moneymore (muine Mór: Big Thicket) in County Londonderry is a plantation town belonging to the Draper's company. In their enthusiasm for improving their property, in 1760 they removed the ancient castle which was, by general agreement, believed to be 'one of the most perfect in Ireland'. Nearby stands the manor of Springhill, now in the care of the National Trust.

It is a friendly and welcoming house, standing amid quiet green acres with an old walled garden and the scent of roses on the air. The Trust have cared for the house and lands since 1957, and it has sympathetically and sensitively been preserved. Over the past thirty years hundreds of visitors from all over the world have climbed its steps and entered its shady and pleasant vestibule. It continues to feel like a home, as indeed it still is to the custodian and his family.

The family who had lived here were called Lenox-Conyngham. Originally the Conynghams had come from Scotland to take possession of Springhill in the reign of James I. Being Protestant and anti-Catholic to a man, they fought both for Cromwell and King William III 'of pious and glorious memory'. They were primarily soldiers and had raised their own troops and had fought for their sovereign on countless occasions, from the bleakness of the Crimea to the blood-spattered mud of Flanders' field. Much later the name was to become Lenox-Conyngham, and the family lived here until the 1950s.

Once it had been a fortified manor house, well equipped to withstand any assault of its enemies, but today those fortifications have largely disappeared, save for the great barn. The house is in white, rough cast stone with two broad and attractive wings branching from the main house. Beside the house, though not too close, still stand those essential offices required by every country squire: laundry, dairy, dovecote and stables. In the walled garden where once the ladies of the house would repair with their needlework there still grows the famous 'McCartney Rose', named after Lord McCartney, one time ambassador to the Imperial Court of China. Its scent lingers on the air to blend with lavender, camomile, and all the scents of the herb garden.

It is a lived in house with bric-a-brac and well-thumbed books on its shelves, together with family portraits and photographs, and the large and commodious furniture of earlier days. It is precisely because it is a family house, with a light and dark patterning woven over the centuries, that Springhill has its own aura of mystery about it. However, one would hesitate to call it a 'haunted house', a phrase that, thanks to the often misleading and lurid connotations attached, would conjure up a totally erroneous picture of Springhill.

While the house has been a family residence for over 300 years, not until 1832 was there any record of it being 'haunted'. If earlier generations heard or saw anything unusual, they certainly did not speak about it. The trigger for paranormal happenings seems to have been the death in 1816 of George Lenox-Conyngham, who died by his own hand in the Blue Bedroom at the front of the house. Mina Lenox-Conyngham, one of his latter day descendants, recorded in her fascinating book *An Old Ulster House* the comment written into the family Bible by his second wife, Olivia: 'George Lenox Conyngham being in a very melancholy state of mind for many months prior, put an end to his existence by pistol shot. He lingered from the 20th November 1816 to the 22nd, and died, thanks to Almighty God, a truly penitent Christian. He was in the 64th year of his age. Buried at Lissan.' Lissan refers to another family estate close by.

The reason for his 'melancholy' seems unclear, but it may have something to do with Olivia who, if one is to believe contemporary reports, was a less than sympathetic and loving wife, although she was a devoted mother. She followed George to the grave in 1832. The first 'curious events' seem to date from about this time. One occupier of the Blue Bedroom, the Hon. Andrew Stuart, George's son-in-law, would find that, when he awoke in the morning, the clothes that he had disposed tidily on a chair the previous night had now 'migrated' to another chair!

The family entertained a great deal, and often Springhill would be full of family and friends. In 1888 a Miss Wilson, who was a close friend of the elder daughter of the house, Millie, was staying in another bedroom, known as the Cedar Room. This room is situated halfway up the main staircase of the house and is now furnished as a day nursery. The two girls had sat up exchanging confidences in this room until quite late one night. At last Millie had said 'Goodnight' and retired to her own room on the first floor. After she had gone, Miss Wilson discovered that Millie had left her diary behind and, knowing that her friend would have need of the book, hurried out onto the landing to take it up to her. As she did so, she saw in the bright moonlight streaming through the landing window a tall woman, whom she did not recognize at the time, standing on the upper landing. The woman seemed most distressed and hurried across the landing to the door of the Blue Bedroom, whereupon she flung her hands in the air and promptly vanished. Later Miss Wilson was to recognize her from a portrait, as Olivia Lenox-Conyngham.

Perhaps it was this same lady who came to see two small boys who were sleeping in the Blue Bedroom many generations later. They told their nurse that 'a lady stood at the mantelpiece and talked to them'. The children did not seem at all disturbed, and it was obvious she had not frightened them. This would indeed tie in with what was known of Olivia and her great love of children. Singlehandedly she nursed a family of six through the dreaded smallpox. In the 1980s, another child told of a 'grey lady' who touched her on the arm while she was on the upper landing. One or two of the children in the family also mentioned 'a gentleman in a cloak' in the Blue Room who, it seemed, they did not like one bit!

A very curious manifestation took place in this room in the last decade of the nineteenth century. Again it involved a visitor, a Miss Hamilton. One morning she came down to breakfast, a little pale and obviously upset. Upon enquiry from her hostess, she told of the night's events. Mina Lenox-Conyngham records this in her book: 'I had gone to bed in the great four poster bed and the fire had died down and I had begun to be drowsy when it suddenly seemed that the room was full of excited people – servants I thought – who were pushing and wrangling in whispers. I felt overcome by fear, but then I heard a clicking sound behind me, as though a door had been opened, and then a light shone at my back, and someone seemed to come through this light and still the commotion, so all fear left me, and after a while I fell asleep ...'

Charlotte, her hostess, looked thoughtful, for what Miss Hamilton could not have known was that there was a door hidden behind the canopy of the bed, that had been papered over some considerable time before. In recent times, when the door was once again opened, it led to a small powder closet, and in it were found a pair of gloves and a bag of bullets.

One must conjecture as to this manifestation also surrounding Olivia Conyngham. Why it should be she that haunts the Blue Room and not her husband, the suicide, provides food for thought. One suggestion is that, particularly in the case of suicide, those close to the victim may feel remorseful and guilty for what they may see as their own 'sins of omission'. Hence, they may haunt in an attempt to redress the balance.

There have been other minor disturbances in the house, both in the kitchens and on the main stairs. Footsteps in the attics have also been heard, and there is scarcely a custodian of the house who has not had some strange experiences. The author, while doing research in Springhill many years ago, was sitting alone in the Cedar Room with the door onto the main stair on the latch. Suddenly, light footsteps were heard outside and the heavy door swung back, but no one came in. At the same time the old oak cradle in the room began to move as though some unseen hand was rocking it. There was the sense of a gentle presence in the room.

Springhill is a house worth a visit, for it embraces all that is gracious and lovely in a country home. There is in fact only one place at Springhill that exudes an undefinable sense of dread. It is one of the out offices, which is now used to display items of country life. A very practical man confessed that it was the only place he did not like, for 'the shivers' ran all over him. To date, no explanation can be offered for this mystery.

County Tyrone, affectionately known as 'Tyrone among the bushes' because of its richly wooded southeastern corner, is Northern Ireland's largest county. The Sperrin Mountains cover a large part of the north, while the Slieve Beag range lies to the south on the Fermanagh and Monaghan borders. Two of the finest Georgian mansions in Northern Ireland lie in the county at Caledon and Baronscourt.

It too possesses traditions of the 'black dog'. About a century ago, a small girl spoke of her horrifying experience of having one of these creatures in her bedroom: 'I remember it clearly as though it was last night. I thought that I woke and saw a huge, curly black dog looking at me. Then he came over to the bed with his mouth open, and his great red tongue hanging out. He snuffled and licked my face and hands ...' A similar experience as occurred to the children of Castle Archdale in County Fermanagh.

The young girl grew up and the memory faded until, fifteen years later, she told a male cousin of the experience. To her astonishment she found that he had had a similar experience in the same room. He said that every time he slept in the room the dog arrived to 'greet him'. Furthermore, the dog had a companion, a little old lady!

An unusual and well-documented incident occurred near the border town of Strabane. The town stands where the Rivers Mourne and Finn unite to form the Foyle. A castle built here in James I's time has long since disappeared, but the town is proud of the fact that the town was the birthplace of John Dunlop who, in 1771, published America's first daily newspaper, the '*Pennsylvanian Packet*'.

The experience was described by a Mr William McKay, who told of an event that happened to him on the outskirts of the town in December, 1856. Mr McKay had been out wildfowling and was on his way home when he heard a dog barking fiercely and then, a moment later, a single musket shot. This was followed by a veritable fusillade of shots.

Greatly alarmed by these events, Mr McKay moved cautiously to where there was a clearing in the trees. Almost immediately a fire erupted in the clearing. This struck him as very odd, for while there was no dwelling nearby, McKay had the distinct impression that a house was on fire and he could see burning thatch falling into water.

Then both the fire and the musketry died down and McKay heard the sound of a bugle and the noise of horsemen coming at the canter. These noises too died away and an eerie stillness pervaded the place. Understandably frightened by these events, William McKay hurried home and recounted his experience to his father who, while interested, did not seem surprised. He explained to his son that he was not the first to encounter 'the burning cottage' in the wood, and he recounted this story.

At the end of the seventeenth century a widow called Sally Mackey had lived with her three sons on the outskirts of the piece of land where William McKay had been wildfowling. There had been some hostility between the local militia and the Mackey family, and a company of soldiers from an infantry regiment at Lifford had been sent with a warrant to arrest the brothers for treasonable activities.

The soldiers found that they could only approach the cottage in single file up a bridle path from the main Londonderry road, and while they were negotiating this they were spotted by the Mackey dog, who barked a warning to his masters. A soldier brought the dog down with a single shot. At this the Mackeys opened fire on the troops, killing and wounding several. It was said that the widow Mackey did most of the shooting while her sons re-loaded the muskets.

Then the cottage caught fire, the door was forced open and the widow carried out unconscious through the smoke and flames. Inside the cottage her three sons lay dead. The widow, though suffering from severe burns, lived to tell the tale. A back-up troop of cavalry was sent for from Lifford, but by the time they arrived it was all over. William McKay, nearly 150 years later, heard all these activities in the right chronological order from the single shot that killed the dog to the burning of the cottage. One does wonder whether, in the years between, the surname 'Mackey' had become 'McKay' and that there might have been a connection between the two families. One also wonders whether these aetheric echoes, experienced by a man alone as he travelled homeward, were the result of some ability of his subconscious mind to 'tune in' to past events. Indeed, if there were blood ties between one generation and another could he have inherited memories of the event that suddenly surfaced in his conscious mind? One interesting sidelight lends more mystery. From the behaviour of McKay's dog it seems that it too participated in the experience and exhibited extreme terror. Did the dog 'perceive' these events on his own, or was he picking up vibrations from his master?

Another instance of that curious phenomenon known as the 'hungry grass' occurred in County Tyrone near the county town of Omagh. It concerned a summer visitor to the county, who was taking a cycling holiday in the early 1920s. He had been enjoying the hospitality of farm houses and cottages along his route around Ulster and stopped for the night at a small farm cottage about ten miles from Omagh. His landlady was a pleasant soul in her sixties, and he was delighted to find that she knew quite a bit about local history and places of interest. The cottage nestled at the foot of a hill which was crowned by what appeared to be the ruin of a small church or chapel, and Mr Reid determined to stroll up after supper and take a look. His landlady told him that it attracted some small attention on account of a fine medieval archway over the main door.

When supper was over, Mr Reid took his way through the

field at the rear of the cottage and up the hill. There was in fact very little to see, but one did get a fine view of the surrounding countryside from the top of the hill. Quite pleased with his gentle stroll, Mr Reid descended the hill towards the cottage. About half way down the hill, he began to feel giddy and nauseous. Then, quite suddenly, he was seized with the most horrific hunger pangs and stomach cramps, so vicious in fact that he fell to his knees. Half crawling, half stumbling he struggled on towards the back wall of the cottage, quite convinced that he was dying. Through all the pain and discomfort he had the eerie sensation that he was not alone, but that someone was following him down off the hill.

Finally he reached the wall and hauled himself upright against it, trembling all over as the hunger pangs tore at him. Fortunately his hostess was in the garden and, seeing his plight, ran to help him. She half-carried, half-dragged him into the cottage. On the table was a freshly baked batch of scones and wheaten bread. To her astonishment, her guest grabbed a fistful of the bread and stuffed it into his mouth. He then proceeded to demolish most of what she had baked. With dawning comprehension, the woman hurried to the scullery and fetched a pitcher of buttermilk with which Mr Reid proceeded to wash down the bread and scones. Slowly the colour came back in his cheeks and the shivering stopped, but his hostess could see that he was both frightened and confused. She tried to explain to him about 'the hungry grass'. When she was a child her mother, who had lived in the same cottage, had told her about the first time she had seen someone attacked by the 'fear gortagh'. 'It seems, Mr Reid,' she said, 'that many years ago, during the Great Famine, many wretched folk lay down and died where they fell from starvation. They had existed for days perhaps on leaves and berries and even grass. An old superstition says that wherever that poor soul lay down to die, the grass took up his hunger, so that if anyone should happen to step on it at that spot then he too would be seized with the terrible hunger pangs. The only cure was to do what you have just done: get as much food into you as soon as possible.'

Since Mr Reid was a schoolteacher there was no need to explain the rigours of the Great Famine to him; but what he had experienced seemed as unbelievable as it was bizarre. He found it very hard to come to terms with, despite the assurances of his hostess that it had happened to others from time to time. Then he frowned as he recalled something else. 'Did you see the lad,' he asked, 'standing in the field as you helped me through the gate?' His hostess looked puzzled. 'There was no one in the field,' she assured him, 'except ourselves.' Mr Reid shook his head, for just as he had dragged himself to the garden wall he had seen a young boy, with a torn coat and ragged breeches, standing alone in the field. He would never forget the face of that child, for it was thin and racked with pain. Then, as he was helped into the garden, the child had grown indistinct and vanished. The woman of the house crossed herself. 'God care for the poor soul,' she said. 'God send him to his rest.' And stout Protestant that he was, Mr Reid echoed that prayer.

It is some years since I have had reports about the 'hungry grass' though some of the older generation, in areas hardest hit by the famine, would recollect tales told to them by parents of the 'fear gortagh'. One old lady in Cavan, celebrating her ninety-first year, told a folklore researcher that the plague of the 'hungry grass' had been so virulent near her mother's home that a loaf of bread and a pitcher of milk were always kept beside the door for emergencies!

14 The Realm of the Faerie

There has never been a time when mankind has not believed in or had contact with the realm of the faerie. No matter how far we have come along the path of cold logic and the mundane matters of what we are accustomed to regard as the 'real world', there has always been that shadowy glimpse of a world apart, a world of mist and shadow, peopled by sights, sounds and beings who have an affinity with us yet are not of our kind. This is true, of course, the whole world over and not merely in Ireland, although the Celtic peoples of Europe have stronger ties than most with what Dermot McManus, one of Ireland's greatest students of fairylore, was pleased to call 'The Middle Kingdom'.

In writing this book it seems that there are three strands of this most enchanting of lands: first, there is the mystery and lure of the natural world of earth and river, of flora and fauna and the shaping of mountain and forest. Then there is the mystery of the human personality, the strange ways of man in his own particular circumstances which may leave its mark long after the individual has gone; these are the joys and tragedies of man's destiny. Lastly, there is that mysterious world that hovers about both – a middle world, a third dimension peopled by beings that have existed since the world began. Some of the world's peoples have close ties with this third thread; others have forgotten or lost much of the wisdom of the old ways – and now it is too late, for they are past recall. Yet it is a mercy that bards, poets and ordinary folk have seen fit to preserve the knowledge of times past in the songs and stories that have been passed down from generation to generation. Even the most prosaic of us know in our hearts that there is a grain of truth at the root of all the wonders and mysteries spoken of from time immemorial.

Intermingled with tales of heroic deeds and high magic are the threads of faith and religious belief, from the Druidic cult far back to the ancient faiths that preceded the Druids. The belief in the faerie is relevant to our spiritual and psychical development and to the universal memory of our race. In early times 'the faerie' was thought to be a great and powerful spirit, more like us in face and form, than the gentle sprites one reads about in fairy tales. They were not, as some believed, representations of the human dead but beings alive and powerful in both the Middle Kingdom and in the world of man.

The question remains: what are 'the faeries'? In Irish terms they are called Sluagh Sidhe – 'the people of the mounds' – a race of living beings familiar with the natural elements of our world: earth, air, fire and water. In early Christian times it was believed that the faeries were angels who had fallen from grace and yet, while flawed and perverse, not so damned as to be cast into the Pit. They possessed degrees of good and evil so that the 'bad faerie' displayed his 'badness' by how he looked and behaved and the degree of malevolence he displayed towards man. The 'good faeries' endeavoured to perform acts of kindness and happiness. Still, whether good or bad, all were aware that they had lost their chance of Heaven and, unlike man, could not be redeemed.

The faeries have a hierarchy that extends from the great host of the sidhe down to the smallest, most mischievous elves and leprechauns, the shy forest nymphs and the gentle water faeries. They are as divergent in their achievements and ways of life as human beings. They differ greatly in physical terms too, from the tall and graceful sidhe to the tiny beings of woodland and meadow. All over our planet there are numerous varieties of 'the little people' or 'the gentry' as they are called, although the names they are known by can be as varied and numerous as one can imagine, from the shores of the Black Sea to the green land of Ireland.

Although in the four provinces of Ireland there is a large variety of faeries, in general terms the island possesses two main kinds: the 'trooping faeries' or 'faerie host', and the 'solitary faerie'. Both have their own tasks and ways of behaviour that have become familiar to us through song and story, and more rarely by personal encounter.

It is difficult to talk of their behaviour in terms of 'right' or 'wrong', or indeed to think of them in moral terms at all. The sidhe live for the moment. They use mortals as seems most expedient, and their actions towards human beings are not geared to consideration as to what is best for them but what seems appropriate in a particular situation. They do have certain rules and ways of going about our world and their own and are fastidious creatures, sensitive to small acts of kindness and scrupulous in remembering a slight or rewarding a kindness. Above all they prefer to be left alone, and while in certain circumstances they will consort with humans they are at all times a reclusive and shy race.

Perhaps it is important to pause and wonder where this magical race, so much a part of Ireland's mysterious beginnings, came from. It is said that they descended from the Tuatha De Danaan, a god-like race that came from Greece, and they contended with the inhabitants of Ireland – 'the sons of Mil, the Milesians from whom the latterday Irish descended'. So humankind and immortals vied with each other and in the end 'the sons of Mil' prevailed and a compromise was struck that allowed the Milesians to rule 'above ground' while the immortal Tuatha De Danaan would hold sway underground and in water. Thus they compromised and Ireland had the best of both worlds in a co-existent 'golden age'. But over the years the two races drew apart, although there would always be some contact between 'the gods' who became 'the sidhe' and the race of mortals. The sidhe, retaining their most 'angelic' quality, that of immortality, were always to command awe and respect from mortals, while for their own part mortals could attain heavenly status by grace and sacrifice and had the gifts of love and compassion. The faeries, to their eternal regret, could never attain Heaven. The theological status of the faerie in the Almighty's scheme of things has always been fraught with confusion and misunderstanding, and it is a subject best left to wiser heads than mine.

> 'How beautiful they are,
> The lordly ones
> That dwell in the hills,
> In the hollow hills.'

So sang the poet, for indeed the sidhe dwell in the green raths and mounds of the quiet places in Ireland and in general keep their dwellings close to Mother Earth. Few mortals have seen the inside of a faerie rath, except for the rare few who are invited in, or some innocent who stumbles upon one by accident. Like all homes, they are a matter of personal choice, and faerie tastes can be quite extravagant, with gold and silver, shining crystal and finely woven drapes. At least this is what is *said* to be displayed if we are to believe those mortals allowed to view the dwelling of the faerie. One has to remember that once a mortal has left the home of the sidhe, he may have some difficulty recollecting exactly what he has witnessed – especially since, if one stops in a faerie dwelling, it can be such an enchanting experience that what one thinks of as a single night could well turn out to be a hundred years. There is also the problem of what you *think* you see. Some critics of the faerie race will declare that human beings who are under a spell of enchantment will be made to see what the faeries *want* them to see and that, in reality, the gold and silver trinkets are really rotting lumps of clay and wood and that the 'palace' is a dark and malodorous hole in the ground.

There are places other than raths that the little people frequent, including the areas around certain trees and bushes, where they are wont to hold their revels. In particular instances, streams and pools can be the gathering places. One favourite spot is under a hawthorn bush or tree, and in the Irish countryside fairy thorns or 'skeaghs' abound.

The fairy thorn is a distinctive tree standing alone in a field. The 'lone bush' is often twisted and gnarled with age and has an ominous appearance. No man in his right mind will set a hand to it, either to cut it down or to burn it, for to do so will incur the dreadful wrath of the faerie.

In 1965 the author spoke to a woman in Mourne Mountain country, which is powerful fairy country. She showed me a fairy thorn in the field next to the farmhouse. Her young grand-daughter was playing with a stick and a stone in the field until, with an exclamation of horror, the granny realized that the child had broken the stick off the thorn tree. With a muttered apology, she excused herself and disappeared out through the back kitchen. From there she crossed the field to the child. She took the stick from the child's hand and, with a length of linen, carefully bound the stick back onto the tree; as she did this I could see that she was speaking aloud but could not hear what it was she said. Then she led the child three times around the tree, before delivering a good smack to the fat little legs, whereupon the child ran crying into the byre.

Her explanation upon coming into the kitchen was 'that it brought no luck to destroy the little people's property'. She continued, 'Many a time when I was a young girl I would be seeing the little ladies and gentlemen dancing about the tree and it all shimmering and sparkling. My mother, God rest her, would leave bread and milk on May Eve, below the tree, and it was always gone in the morning!'

Today it is still considered wise to leave the fairy tree well alone, even in great halls of learning such as The Queen's University of Belfast, whose grounds are home to a fairy thorn. The plans for the extension of the university some years ago were rapidly modified in order that the little tree should not be sacrificed to architectural requirements. The concept of the thorn being a traditional meeting place of the sidhe is honoured and believed all over Ireland. Holy Thorns and Holy Wells go together in the beliefs of both the Christian and the Elder Faiths. In other parts of the world too there are connections between the power of the fairy tree and the older faith. The honouring of the Holy Thorn that one finds at Glastonbury in England is an example. There the legend has it that the Holy Thorn grew from the staff of Saint Joseph of Arimathea, and on this holy and most magical site there still grows a thorn that flowers at Christmastime. In Ireland, as Christianity superceded the earlier faith, the sites of fairy thorns were often married to the siting of a Holy Well, of which, at one time, Ireland possessed three thousand.

In company with raths, lisses and duns (names given to faerie forts and habitats), there are few locations more venerated and associated with the faerie than the thorn tree. The white thorn tree is particularly striking. Other trees held in special significance are the hazel, blackthorn, rowan and ash. These trees are chief among the shrubs and field herbs that are of special importance to the 'little folk' in their daily lives and medicinal work. With the lovely rowan tree there is some difference of opinion. Many believe that this tree is best used against faerie magic and is most effective against witchcraft. Yet others see the rowan as a 'fairy tree'. Popular belief may sometimes turn every lone bush into a 'fairy tree', which may stretch one's credulity, but it suffices to say that there has always been a close affinity between thorns and the faerie.

Dermot McManus, in his fascinating book on The Middle

Kingdom, tells of such a tree that grew in the faerie fort Lis Ard, not far from his own home. It was a neat and sturdy tree, some four foot in height and growing out of a bank on the northern side of the hill. It was in some curious fashion a tree of 'considerable presence and demeanour', and it was well known to folk round about. At one point McManus' grandfather decided that the little tree needed a higher profile and proposed that he should shift the tree to a site in front of the door of the house. This was in the year 1854, and while the idea found increasing favour with the elder McManus, everyone else viewed the shifting of the tree with considerable apprehension. Finally, thoroughly exasperated at the non-cooperation he was getting, the grandfather upped and shifted it himself. Much to everyone's astonishment, the tree survived its removal to new quarters and flourished. One has to say that the McManuses themselves were not so fortunate. Over the next decade the farm ailed and money became scarce. These misfortunes were laid at the root of the fairy tree, and many a wish was expressed that the tree would be returned to its proper place.

As Dermot McManus noted, the tree was a great favourite with the birds, especially the so-called 'fairy birds', the robins and the wrens who yearly nursed their families among its branches. There were other venerable trees at Lis Ard: a great and mighty oak and another thorn tree. It was said that on special occasions the faerie folk gathered under the oak at the foot of the hill for dancing and other merriment.

Of course, there are two sides to most faerie matters, and just as Lis Ard abounded with benevolent trees, so there were trees and bushes that simply reeked of malevolence. Here lurked demons and evil spirits, and all things unholy. Naturally, no one in his or her right mind removed so much as a leaf from these trees. It was agreed that three most awful demons lived near to the McManus oak, and they would torment travellers who had the temerity to pass the tree at night. It was noted too that at one time the tree had been attacked with an axe, but no one knew more of the tale. One shudders to think what befell that foolish man who performed such a rash deed!

The range of tales told about the dire effects of moving a fairy thorn are legion and come from all parts of Ireland. In Omagh, County Tyrone, in the 1940s, a contractor had reason to move a fairy thorn on a building site that he owned beside a country road. His workmates urged him to 'leave well alone'. None of his workers would lay a finger on the tree, so he hired two men from a neighbouring townland to 'do the deed'. The men arrived on a motorbike and wasted no time in setting up the tools for the 'execution'. It was all over in a very short time, for after three strokes the tree gave a lurch and, contrary to all expectations, fell onto the back of one of the woodsmen who had gone to fetch a tool from his motorbike. The unfortunate man was found to be dead on arrival at the hospital. The whole idea was dropped and the tree shored up for safety's sake.

There were those, of course, who muttered behind their hands that the builder had not seen fit to explain to the two itinerant workers that it was a fairy tree. Now it was his fault that a man lay dead, because he had angered the faerie folk. The site lay empty for many a year until a stranger came who, with little concern for the ways of the faerie, built a smart new bungalow on the site. Much to everyone's surprise, it came to no harm.

It seems curiously chilling that death and tragedy should come about on the heels of moving a small thorn tree, but there are too many reported incidents over the years to dismiss the allegations out of hand. One hears of a parish priest who needed the removal of a fairy thorn to facilitate the rebuilding of a cottage hospital. Try as he would, none of his devout flock would render him aid. Finally he too had to import labour to come and fell the tree. The tree was despatched and the workman paid and sent home. Some weeks later he succumbed to a stroke from which he never recovered. He was dead within the year, and they 'walked' his coffin to the graveyard just a few yards from the field where the remains of the thorn tree branches and stump could still be seen. The plans for the cottage hospital met with all kinds of problems, so it was never refurbished and eventually it was closed altogether. Finally the field was handed over to the Garda for their use, and the grass grew over the mound where the little tree had been.

We see the faerie as an image of ourselves for the most part, but without blemish or spot. The composition of their forms is not known, so mostly we conclude that they are ethereal beings, capable of 'shape shifting' to suit their purposes, taking on the forms of animals, ancient crones or beautiful young people. They can show anger and joy, generosity and revenge, but they

lack love and compassion. The fact that we mortals have seen
less of them in modern times, may be because we have become
cynical and disbelieving, thus the connecting links between the
races have been destroyed and the mist has come down on our
eyes. The precious 'sight' has vanished, never to return.

The ways of the faerie mirror ours: they dance to perfection,
make love, are fine musicians and enjoy all manner of sport and
entertainment. One specific talent is their superb horsemanship
and they own fine horses, wild white creatures with fire in their
nostrils and their manes tipped with gold. It is a fortunate mortal
that sees the 'host of the sidhe' ride out in the moonlight.

Some years ago, in the Mountains of Mourne, an old man
going home late one May evening beside a well known faerie
path saw the 'hosting of the sidhe', their shining garments
blowing in the wind and the faerie horses galloping above the
blades of grass. 'I was privileged to see,' he told a neighbour,
who found him wandering in a daze in the lane. 'My mother was
a help to a fairy when she was a young girl and 'the gentry' were
good to us,' he explained. His neighbour, no doubt, smiled and
shook his head, until he saw something shining in the grass at
his feet. Bending down, he lifted up a tiny silver horseshoe.

It is not as rare as one might assume to find items of clothing
– shoes, hats or little waistcoats – in country houses the length of
Ireland. These treasures are put away carefully in tissue and
hidden in a drawer, only to be brought out on special occasions
to amaze the stranger. In 1972 farmer Michael O'Shea found a
tiny pair of breeches and a coat on a stone beside a stream. The
breeches were patched and worn, while the waistcoat had a
single silver button. Of course there are those who will smile at
this and shake their heads at the improbable prospect of making
such a find. I would have been among them, had it not been that
in the early 1960s I saw such a waistcoat with my own eyes and
heard the story that went with it. It was told to me by a
Presbyterian minister from Scotland, who was on holiday in the
beautiful Glens of Antrim.

He and the friend he was staying with were returning home in
the car to the house which stood at the head of the Glen. Alec,
as I shall call him, suddenly saw to his astonishment a small man
sitting on a rock at the side of the road, some small distance
away. The wee man seemed to be tying his bootlace. Then,
when he saw that he was being observed, he was up in a flash

and running up the hill among the heather. Alec was astounded but said nothing, for fear of looking foolish. However, they had only travelled a few yards when his friend asked him. 'Did you-er-see anything back there along the road, Alec?' 'I played for time,' said Alec. 'So I said, "Why? What did you see?" ' His friend stopped the car and reversed back a few yards to the point where he had seen the same little man. 'That's it!' he exclaimed. 'I know you'll think I'm havering, but I thought I saw a wee man sitting on that rock.' 'And so did I!' said Alec.

The two men now compared the extent of their individual experiences, and discussed how the wee man had been dressed. According to both he had worn a shirt and waistcoat, with a scarf knotted about his neck, brown breeches and brown boots. On his head was a soft cap. He had seemed elderly but with a cheery face. The two clergymen came to the sheepish conclusion that they had both seen a leprechaun – one of the so-called solitary faeries of Ireland known by the name leprechaun, cluricane, or Lurican (Kerry). This was a type of fairy specializing in shoemaking. By tradition, leprechauns were clever beings with a fondness for hoarding treasure, and to part a leprechaun from his crock of gold was a well nigh impossible task, for once you caught a faerie you must not take your eye off him or he and his treasure would vanish! This solitary faerie is common only to Ireland, and it is indeed unusual to spot a leprechaun as easily as did the two clergy.

Alec went on to say that they had decided to keep quiet about their experience, for what would folk think if two 'men of the cloth' should tell such a tale? 'So why are you telling me?' I asked. 'Well,' said Alec, 'I knew you would believe us, and I was busting to tell someone.'

I wanted to find out the end of Alec's tale. 'What did you see or do then?' I asked. 'Well,' Alec said, 'we got out of the car and walked around for a bit, peering into bushes. Then my friend grabbed my arm and pointed up the hillside. There sitting beside a small rock was the biggest brown hare I have ever seen. For a long moment we stared at one another; then, with a whisk of the legs, the hare was away up the slope. We never saw hare nor wee man again.'

This was not quite the end of the story, for some time later I was sent a cutting by Alec, with the comment that someone had found a tiny waistcoat on the road near to the spot where he had seen the leprechaun. On the back of the cutting Alec had written, 'I wonder, was it his???'

Many places in Ireland give notice that we are treading on ground that has a particular affiliation to faerie kind. The very names given to areas make the connections for us: Lis Ard, Hill of the Fairies, Knock-na-Shee, the Fairy Track, Ard-na-Shee and so on. If one happens to live in or near these places, then one is particular about one's own comings and goings and where one erects one's own dwelling. To build across a faerie path bodes ill. One is much wiser to take note of the lay of the land with reference to the sidhe.

In 1984, in the middle of Mourne Country, I was talking to an elderly farmer whose family had lived in the same farmhouse for over two hundred years. He was an authority on every stick and stone in the district, and in particular was well versed in fairy lore. We stood at his gate and looked down over the mountain as he pointed out items of interest to me. In the far distance, I could see a small stream wending its way through the rocky ground, and there was also, near to a small stone bridge, a cottage. There was no smoke curling from the chimney and the fields about it were deserted. Old Liam followed my sightline. 'It's empty,' he said. 'There's been no one there for over fifty years. The man who built yon house never did himself any good. He had no luck in the place.'

Liam told me how the cottager, despite friendly warnings, had decided to build his cottage on the far side of the bridge, between the water and a strange misshapen rock half way up the hill. By tradition the rock was said to belong to the fairies, and the cottage now stood across the path that was the faeries' right-of-way to the water. 'See?' said Liam. 'The grass is a wee bit greener along the bank, there beside the bridge.' I must confess that I found it hard to distinguish at such a distance, but I nodded encouragingly. Old Liam now told me how the man's cows had been sick more often than not and the lambs had died; the potatoes got mildew and the doctor was forever at the door. It was never said aloud, but the whole countryside knew that the faeries had wished him ill. I enquired as to whether there could have been an amicable solution. Liam spat thoughtfully on the ground and then said: 'He'd have needed to have taken the house down, taken off the gable-end room and gone just ten yards above the rock. But sure, he was told all that. Even then it might not have worked, but he was warned.'

It seemed that money was short and, in any case, the man held little truck with faerie ways. So, after a particularly disastrous season, he simply packed up and moved with his family to Newry. The cottage lay abandoned: no one made any move to buy it or even use it for animals. Year by year it deteriorated until the cottage was overgrown with bramble and briar. 'Sure enough, he had no luck,' Liam reminisced, 'and he took the bad luck with him, for the family had a changeling who never came to anything. She died of the consumption when they went to Newry. I mind she was about fourteen, for I was only a lad meself.'

When a human child was abducted by the faeries, a 'look alike' or 'changeling' was left in its place. This was a fairly common affliction in days gone by. In this case, one must remember that this particular story was only fifty years old. In fact in the early part of 1990, a similar claim of 'a changeling' was made in another part of Mourne, and I had met one or two who claimed to have known the child. In the bad old days, a sickly child was hardly unusual, bearing in mind that poverty and malnutrition abounded. One wonders how many children labelled 'changeling' were simply what we would describe nowadays as 'disadvantaged'. An unfortunate child to whom this label was attached found his or her life to be a living hell, as they were abused and shunned by all.

Certainly, there were authenticated cases that some of the so-called 'changeling' children did exhibit extraordinary gifts of healing and herbalism, as well as an affinity with animals. Mostly they bore some handicap or disabling feature and were seldom beautiful; often their lives were pitifully short. By tradition, boys were taken when very small infants but girls were left a little longer, so that the faeries might choose the prettiest. An unbaptized infant ran the greatest risk of all.

There were several methods of 'persuading' the changeling to go away. One barbaric method was to place the changeling on a red hot shovel and throw it into the fire, or drop it into a manure pit. The fairies would then return the human child, it was believed.

In quiet and mysterious places all over Ireland one may hear of that ancient spirit form the 'Pooka', one of the best known inhabitants of the Middle Kingdom and one which a great number of travellers will vouch for. The spirit takes only animal form and may be seen as a horse, an ass, a goat or, according to Yeats, an eagle. It is mostly black in colour with blazing eyes, and obviously it has some affinity with 'the black dog'. In the Irish the word 'puc' means a male goat. The English Puck is a more endearing earth spirit, funloving, mischievous and quite unlike the Pooka, who brings with him malevolence and death. In Ulster counties, the Pooka is more often described as a black pony with a shaggy mane and burning eyes. Occasionally his exploits take the form of 'treating' some unfortunate to a wild and terrifying ride.

Many places bear the name of the Pooka as an indication that he abides in the district. There is a beautiful waterfall in County Wicklow called Poulaphuca (the Pool of the Púca). Where names include 'rath' or 'Lis', there also may he be found. It is believed that if in the time about Hallowe'en the Puca breathes on the blackberries, they will prove to be inedible.

Its stalking grounds are varied. Pookas frequent river banks and streams, as well as ancient tracks. They appear to have no particular worries about manifesting in broad daylight, nor are they bothered about who sees them. The Pooka is one of the older of the earth spirits, which manifests throughout the thirty-two counties.

One well known Pooka was seen in County Mayo near Pontoon. A local resident was taking her dog for a walk when she saw from a distance what she thought at first was a dark coloured donkey lying in the road. As she drew nearer she could see that it was a very large black dog. It is a tradition that Pookas can 'shape shift', and the form of a black dog is a very common one. As she drew nearer the animal got up and moved to the side of the road, to a grass verge. Then, to her consternation, it simply disappeared. The behaviour of her own dog was interesting. Normally well prepared to stand up for itself in front of strangers, on seeing the creature on the verge the dog began to whine and crept belly to ground in between its mistress and the wall, where it remained until the Pooka vanished.

A sighting that was reported in County Down concerned a farmer taking home two heifers along a quiet lane. As he came down the narrow road, to his utter astonishment a black pony quite literally flew over the hedge into the lane and then cleared the opposite hedge in one gigantic leap. The farmer described it as about fourteen hands high, jet black with a shaggy mane and tail. It made no sound, unlike the heifers, who stampeded off, bawling loudly. Having taken advice, the farmer was in no doubt that he had seen the local Pooka. This all happened in broad daylight and the man concerned was as shrewd and level-headed as they come, which gives one food for thought.

So many books have been written about the mysterious and intriguing Faerie Faith, that this can provide only a small glimpse of it. Whether one wishes to take this particular strand of mysterious Ireland seriously or not, one cannot fail to be intrigued by the wealth of information gathered over the years. Tales of the faerie meet and mingle with information about apparitions and poltergeists, haunted castles and haunted people. Those of us who live in Ireland know that we live in a mysterious, ancient land, whose griefs and tragedies have been many over the centuries and have become wrapped in veils of time. It is easy to dismiss such mysteries as figments of overactive imagination or plain fantasy, but it seems to me to be more worthwhile to cultivate an open mind. Then, perhaps, we shall learn more about our fascinating and mysterious universe than we ever thought possible.

Bibliography

A.A. Illustrated Road Book of Ireland (A.A. Pub., 1963).

Bianconi, M.O'C., *Bianconi* (Hodges Figgis, 1962).

Byrne, Patrick, *Irish Ghost Stories* (Mercier Press, 1991).

Dunne, John, *Haunted Ireland* (Appletree Press, 1977).

Gregory, Lady, *Visions and Beliefs, Vols 1&2* (G.B. Putnam, 1920).

Holzer, Hans, *The Lively Ghosts of Ireland* (Wolfe Publishing, 1967).

MacManus, D.A., *The Middle Kingdom* (Max Parrish, 1959).

O'Donnell, E., *Banshee* (Sands and Co.)

Seymour and Neligan, *True Irish Ghost Stories* (Hodges Figgis, 1969).

St. Clair, Sheila, *Psychic Phenomena in Ireland* (Mercier Press, 1972).

St. Clair, Sheila, *The Step on the Stair* (Glendale Press, 1989).

Index